Shamefully Vanished
A Memoir of a Girl Out of Control

Shamefully Vanished
A Memoir of a Girl Out of Control

Shamefully Vanished
A Memoir of a Girl Out of Control

Shamefully Vanished
A Memoir of a Girl Out of Control

Shamefully Vanished
A Memoir of a Girl Out of Control

Shamefully Vanished
A Memoir of a Girl Out of Control

© 2020 Lena Ma

Shamefully Vanished
A Memoir of a Girl Out of Control

Shamefully Vanished
A Memoir of a Girl Out of Control

All rights reserved. No part of this publication may be reproduced, distributed, or transmitted in any form or by any means, including photocopying, recording, or other electronic or mechanical methods, without the prior written permission of the publisher, except in the case of brief quotations embodied in critical reviews and certain other noncommercial uses permitted by copyright law.

Cover Design by Covers by Combs

Shamefully Vanished
A Memoir of a Girl Out of Control

Shamefully Vanished
A Memoir of a Girl Out of Control

Table of Contents

Chapter One
Will This Ever End?
13

Chapter Two
The Tipping Point
19

Chapter Three
When It All Began
29

Chapter Four
My Anorexia Story
35

Chapter Five
Obsession and Failure
41

Chapter Six
Bulimia Begins
52

Shamefully Vanished
A Memoir of a Girl Out of Control

Chapter Seven
The Time I Almost Died
59

Chapter Eight
To Vomit or Not to Vomit?
69

Chapter Nine
Why Did I Confess?
77

Chapter Ten
Kicked Out and Broke
82

Chapter Eleven
First Residential Experience
88

Chapter Twelve
Getting Worse
95

Chapter Thirteen
I Watched Someone Die
101

Chapter Fourteen
Second Residential Experience
106

Shamefully Vanished
A Memoir of a Girl Out of Control

Chapter Fifteen
Chugging and Change
110

Chapter Sixteen
My Living Hell
116

Chapter Seventeen
The Phase Never Ended
127

Chapter Eighteen
Shame
135

Chapter Nineteen
Mind-Body Disconnection
142

Chapter Twenty
Keeping Secrets
148

Shamefully Vanished
A Memoir of a Girl Out of Control

Shamefully Vanished
A Memoir of a Girl Out of Control

Chapter One
Will This Ever End?

I am confused. Lost. Imprisoned inside this body I no longer have control over. I used to believe that I had my life in my own control, measuring every calorie, every ounce, and every pound that traveled in and out of me.

The perfection and the power that used to rush over me now drown in swift and shallow waves, as I watch the girl I once was vanish with every flush.

Shamefully Vanished
A Memoir of a Girl Out of Control

On the outside, I am aware of the actions I engage in. I know my behaviors are out of the ordinary, dangerous, and ill. I am able to see the damage and pain I am imposing on my body, and I want nothing more than to just stop, than to just experience one day, one moment, where my mind is not constantly bombarded with thoughts of how much I have eaten and how much weight I still have to lose.

I feel this drive pulling me toward a direction that only hurts me and refuses to stop until I lose it all, until I have nothing left except for skin and bones, until I become nothing. I no longer have a say over my actions.

My mind becomes convoluted with one single motive, the motive to binge and purge and nothing else, despite how much it isolates me from my loved ones. I want it to stop.

Every time I swallow without tasting what I put inside my mouth, I feel my throat closing and my body pushing back up what refuses to go down. Every time I force what is half-chewed and eaten to come up, I feel my heart pressing up against my chest, driving me to the point of blacking out.

I fear whether I am going to wake up every morning as I go to sleep at night. I am terrified of touching food or putting food into my mouth because I know I will not be able to enjoy it or keep it down.

One single taste quickly escalates into inhaling everything in sight, struggling to swallow with tears pouring out. Whenever I fall asleep, I fear I may never wake up as I experience endless palpitations and abnormal beating.

Some days I feel better than others, stronger and more motivated to tackle my recovery, but the urge is far more powerful than the will, as my mind constantly loses the battle against my body at every fight.

Why can't it just be simple? I can't remember the last time I went out for a nice dinner without having running thoughts of, "You're going to get fat if you eat this," "You better throw it up if you want to put this inside your mouth," or, "You don't deserve to eat because you ate too much yesterday."

I become drained from wanting things but not allowing myself to have them, wanting to stop the constant purging because I see what it does to my hair and teeth, becoming jealous when others have self-control over what they do or do not eat while I don't, and wanting recovery but fearing how my weight will shift as a result of it.

I just want to eat a normal meal, just once, without calculating the total calorie count inside my head because I haven't had an experience like that since I was a little girl.

I want to be able to choose a restaurant based solely on the types of food they serve and what I'm in the mood for rather than looking up menus beforehand and choosing the restaurant based on my diet plan.

Shamefully Vanished
A Memoir of a Girl Out of Control

I want to be able to wake up one morning and not pace back and forth for hours deciding on whether I should eat, how much I should eat, how fast I should be eating, and if I would be able to purge afterward if I do eat.

I want to stop worrying about whether eating a small bowl of cereal will spiral into eating an entire box of cereal, and I want to stop proportioning my solids to liquids ratio so my meals come up easier.

I want to stop drenching everything I eat with hot sauce and chili pepper flakes so the pain in my mouth will steer me away from wanting to eat more, and I want to stop boiling every item that resembles food just so I have something to binge and purge on, regardless of what it is and what it tastes like.

I am tired of not allowing myself to fulfill my nutritional needs. What began as a simple diet, a simple desire of wanting to lose five pounds so I would get noticed again, quickly ascended into a reflex of throwing up whenever I eat.

I have done this so many times, for so long, sometimes purging up to thirty times a day, that it has become easier to hide. It has gotten to the point where I am skilled at throwing up inside my mouth and spitting it out when no one is looking, a skill that many bulimics strive for, but also a skill that keeps us trapped in the disease that much longer.

For those with eating disorders, the "better" you become at it, the more difficult it becomes to escape. The feeling of knowing that you have mastered control over something that you are able to keep a secret for so long, makes you forget that you are stuck inside a psychological disease.

Shamefully Vanished
A Memoir of a Girl Out of Control

Chapter Two
The Tipping Point

"You never forget your most traumatic moments."

As much as you try to escape from the burdens of your past, they always come back to haunt you the minute you stop to catch a breath. It has taken me ten years, ten years since my eating disorder began, to finally come out and say that I am no longer ashamed to publicize my past.

I can distinctly remember two major downfalls, among many, during my downhill struggle with Bulimia

Shamefully Vanished
A Memoir of a Girl Out of Control

Nervosa. One of them was the night I bought five boxes of Butterscotch Krimpets from the cheap and expired local grocery store about seven blocks away from my university. I left my dorm building one night, with an empty backpack in the middle of a snowstorm, and walked to the store, with my hood up and my hair over my face to avoid being seen, rather than studying for a next-day exam.

Embarrassed and ashamed of even being seen in the food aisle by strangers, I grabbed all five boxes and began heading toward the checkout line. While walking, I noticed that someone had opened a container of chocolate chip cookies and left it sitting on a shelf, glaring in my direction. I had never stolen anything before that moment, but the temptation was too powerful to resist.

I didn't care what was in the cookies. I didn't care if someone had poisoned them. I only cared about stuffing my face with them. I grabbed the open container, checked to make sure there were no cameras, and dumped the remnants into my backpack, spilling crumbs onto the floor, and threw the empty container behind a few loaves of bread.

I paid for the Krimpets and immediately after, I sat on the curb outside the store, opened the boxes, and poured the packaged cakes out into my backpack to avoid carrying five boxes of cakes around and looking guilty. This way, I could hide my shame AND have less trash to deal with later. Win, win!

I went around to the back of the building, threw the empty boxes away into the frozen bushes behind the

Shamefully Vanished
A Memoir of a Girl Out of Control

store, and ran back to my dorm, famished, as my stomach growled from not having eaten all day. As I ran, I dreamt of binging on these delicious cakes in my dorm room and purging them up in the private bathroom I shared with my dorm mates.

However, when I opened the door, my heart sank as I saw my roommate watching movies on her bed, spoiling my plan. I hated her! I couldn't binge with her sitting there; it'll give me away. Smiling weakly at her, I backed out of the room, panicking. My stomach was churning, and I needed to eat. I had been starving myself all day just for this moment, and the only focus and motivation I had was on trying to find somewhere private where I could binge on these cakes all at once.

Whenever I binge, I have to eat everything in one go, at one place. I won't allow myself to eat one cake at a time while trying to find a place to eat the rest. If I did that, the calories would begin digesting quicker. Larger quantities of food make the stomach work harder to push everything down, giving me more time to push them back up.

I bolted down five flights of stairs to the lobby of my building, where I saw a bunch of guys playing pool. Hiding my face, hoping that would conceal my identity, I ran past them and into the communal bathrooms inside the lobby, locked myself inside the handicapped stall, without a care if someone who was actually handicapped had to use it.

I unzipped my backpack and began unwrapping the cakes, one by one, shoving each one into my mouth and swallowing them whole without chewing. Chewing and tasting only wasted time as I was desperate to polish them all off before someone walked in and caught me in the act.

Cake after cake, I shoved into my mouth, choking as I tried to swallow more than I could handle. I stuffed the empty wrappers back inside my backpack after each one to hide the evidence.

When all the Krimpets were gone, I was ready to purge. However, I realized that I forgot my water bottle in my room and needed something to moisten these dry cakes so they would come up easier. I tried heaving them up, but I only ended up coughing and tearing as the dryness put a strain on my throat.

I have learned early on during my bulimic episodes that liquid is the best way to help with purging. I tried purging again. Only saliva came up this time. I tried putting my fingers down my throat, only to end up choking and coughing again.

Desperate and afraid one more cough will grab the attention of the guys outside, I walked out of the stall, fished through the trash can, found a used and empty water bottle, and filled it up with tap water. I walked back into the stall, chugged the water, and purged.

I had purged enough times to know that not everything comes up with just one purge. I walked back out to the sink, filled up the bottle again, walked back into the stall, chugged, and purged again.

Shamefully Vanished
A Memoir of a Girl Out of Control

I repeated this three more times, puking up stomach acid during the last, before I finally confirmed that most, if not all, of the Butterscotch Krimpets were out of my stomach.

Unraveling some toilet paper, I wiped the remnants of vomit from my chin, flushed the toilet, walked out of the stall, and looked in the mirror. My face had become red and swollen from the pressure, my eyes bloodshot from burst veins, and tears streamed down my puffy cheeks.

***

My other memorable instance was the moment that ruined my college education and my hopes for a successful and thriving career. During the annual football game against my university's rival, while everyone else was prepping for the big event, I was ordering pizzas from Dominos, six large pies, if I remembered correctly, ranging from pepperoni to mushroom to plain cheese.

While everyone else was pre-gaming for the game, I was pre-gaming for my three nights straight of binging and purging since my dorm mates were all going to be gone. I was ecstatic to have the entire apartment all to myself. I was thrilled to finally be able to lay out all my junk food and leave my trash everywhere without having to worry about hiding anything from my roommates.

Pretending to be asleep while everyone got ready to leave so I could avoid interacting with them, I placed my Dominos order under my covers, to be delivered exactly 15-minutes after everyone leaves. I swear I could feel my

Shamefully Vanished
A Memoir of a Girl Out of Control

heart skip a beat when I heard a knock on the door and smelled the delicious fragrance from a couple feet away.

I opened the door and grabbed the pizza boxes with brutal strength, as if my life depended on eating this food. I didn't even bother to tip. I never tipped. Tipping meant less money for my next binge and purge session.

I opened all six boxes and aligned them neatly on the couch that I shared with my dorm mates. I then went underneath my bed and pulled out my suitcase full of chips and cookies from the Dollar Store, some of which were expired, but I didn't care.

I also fished through my trash can, found an empty 2-liter soda bottle from nights before, filled it up with tap water, and placed both my snacks and my water out next to the pizzas.

Next, I popped in a movie on my laptop, and I began my binging session, stopping every 30-minutes to throw up in the bathtub when my stomach could no longer hold any more food.

Living with roommates, I had learned that throwing up in the toilet can get too loud and messy, and I can only feign being drunk so many times before people started to catch on. I also learned that throwing up in the toilet causes too much splash back from the disgusting toilet and vomit water, so much to the point where I had to waste toilet paper, piling them up in the toilet bowl to absorb the liquid vomit.

Shamefully Vanished
A Memoir of a Girl Out of Control

However, by throwing up in the bath tub, I can simply pretend to shower, use the running water as a sound mask, use soap and shampoo to mask the smell, and watch all the food, all the calories, all the self-hatred, wash down the drain, without anyone suspecting a thing. However, that particular night was different. My routine of binging, purging, and cleansing did not go as planned. Usually when I binge on pizza, I would attempt to purge after polishing off just one, as one large pie is usually more than enough to fill my stomach to the brim.

But I was starving that night. I hadn't eaten all day, and the food that I ate the night before had all been purged, purged to the point where I felt stomach acid abrasively coming into contact with my teeth.

There is a big difference between "regular purging" and "extreme purging." Regular purging resembles that of purging while drunk. You only purge enough to make yourself feel better and are fully aware that there is still food left inside your stomach. All that ever comes up with regular purging is half-digested food and about a cup of saliva.

However, with extreme purging, you feel like you are about to die. Extreme purging means purging as many times as possible to ensure that your stomach has been emptied of ALL THE FOOD. This usually includes what I like to call "rinsing."

Rinsing means chugging water repeatedly, allowing the zero-calorie water to disperse between the food inside your stomach, making them easier to come up, and purging up the water with the now-wet food. This ensures

Shamefully Vanished
A Memoir of a Girl Out of Control

a greater chance that you will purge up all the food that was eaten.

This is usually repeated over and over and over until the only thing that seems to come up is acid, water, and saliva. Extreme purging means repeating this three more times, EVEN AFTER acid begins to burn through your intestines, in order to guarantee an empty stomach.

Extreme purging is usually then followed by lightheadedness, tremors, and a slight chance of blacking out, which I like to solve by either engaging in another binge and purge session until one of my extreme purges do not result in shaking, or I simply try to sleep it off.

Back to my story. I devoured three large pizzas that night before attempting to throw them up. Throwing up one pizza is usually difficult enough, as the dough and cheese like to coagulate, forming one large sticky ball inside my stomach, making it close to impossible to throw up without gagging or choking unless I pace myself with enough water in between. However, I failed to pace myself this time and throwing up three pies at once proved to be a nightmare.

After over 40-minutes of gagging and tearing up, I had thrown up roughly 95% of the three pies inside my stomach, with multiple rinses, of course. Looking into the bath tub and seeing a massive pile of chewed up pies gave me a huge sense of satisfaction.

It felt almost like an accomplishment to be able to eat so much, to be able to "taste" the delicious food but not store them as fat inside my body. I felt in control. I felt a sense of power from what I was able to do.

After admiring my "hard work," I attempted to wash it all down, like I have done many times before, only to clog the drain. Fuck. The clumps of dough and cheese were still coagulated in my vomit that my bile clumped up while attempting to go down the drain.

Panicking, I shoved my hand down the gutter to try and pull up some chunks and create an opening. I tried letting the water continue to run to soften the food and catalyze the process of washing the food down.

However, seconds later, the drain began backing up, sending my vomitus back toward my way and causing the water level to begin to rise.

The more I tried to force the chewed up, and now very disgusting, food down the drain, the more the tub kept filling up, water and vomit levels rising and rising until the bath tub overflowed and diluted chunks of vomitus began flowing onto the tiled bathroom floor.

I grabbed all the towels I could find, my dorm mates' included, and a few of my sweaters, and I laid them all out to absorb the liquid. Eventually, I had to turn the water off and shove a sock into the drain to block more water from backing up. The water level eventually stopped rising, and I just sat there, on the vomit covered floor, staring at my bath tub full of shame.

Shamefully Vanished
A Memoir of a Girl Out of Control

Shamefully Vanished
A Memoir of a Girl Out of Control

Chapter Three
When It All Began

As a little girl, I loved to eat. Cookies, cereal, chips, candy, pasta, bread, dried oats, sugar packets, raw dough, pretty much anything and everything that resembled or somewhat resembled food. Food was heaven. Food was comfort. Food was love. Unlike most people who overeat, I didn't eat out of hunger.

I ate, and still eat, out of boredom and loneliness. My parents worked all the time when I was a child, and I was often left alone at home with my brother. There were no

Shamefully Vanished
A Memoir of a Girl Out of Control

set meals, barely any home-cooked food, and I spent most of my days after school at the local convenience store picking up ice cream and chips as my after-school snacks, stockpiling and hiding them in my room as my security net so I could snack on them whenever I wanted company or some love.

Even when my parents were home, I was often ignored and left alone, forcing myself to be my own company. I was not close with my brother, my parents watched TV whenever they were home from work, and I didn't have any friends I could invite over or hang out with.

I still ate normal meals with my family during dinners, but afterward, I always grabbed a box of cereal and snacked on the sugary flakes to provide myself comfort: in the car while going shopping, on the living room couch while watching TV, and sometimes I even grabbed a handful of cereal with me on my way to the bathroom.

Even when I was around my parents and my family, I still always felt like I didn't belong. I felt alone even when I was surrounded by people.

I distinctly remember a time when I was 6-years old and had the chicken pox. My family had bought a box of pepperoni pizza that I wasn't allowed to eat, and instead, I had to settle for plain fish for dinner. Around 3am that night, I snuck down into the kitchen and started picking the pepperoni off the pizza and shoving them into my mouth.

Four pepperonis later, my parents caught me sitting on the kitchen table stuffing my face, grease dripping down

Shamefully Vanished
A Memoir of a Girl Out of Control

my chin. To this day, my family still believes and jokes around that I did what I did because I wasn't allowed to have any of the pizza and that's why I snuck down and ate some in the middle of the night.

However, the truth is, I did what I did because just hours before I snuck down, my mother had hit me with a broom for talking back when I wasn't supposed to. I felt unloved and unwanted by my mother, and I felt as if my brother always had her attention while I always had none.

I couldn't sleep that night, as the loneliness had gotten too strong. I polished off the rest of the snacks I had hidden in my closet, and I was craving for more. After hours of crying, I could still smell the pizza wafting into my room, and I could not stop the temptation, fully believing that nothing else besides that pizza could ease my loneliness and keep me secure and safe.

* * *

Fast forward to four years later, my parents brought me to my pediatrician for my annual checkup, and after I was weighed, my pediatrician laughed at me and proceeded to criticize my parents for feeding me too much as I was 20lbs overweight. I felt ashamed.

My parents became very angry at me, and the endless laughter from my pediatrician made me want to hide.

While I could have very well continued my snacking habits in private, even when my parents put me on a strict diet, the shame that I felt during that moment overpowered me more than my desire to snack for comfort.

I still craved food. I still craved the comfort that came with hoarding food and always having something to chew on. So, I began binging on gum. The chewing movements kept my mouth occupied while also allowing me to burn some needed calories in the process.

Plus, one stick of gum only has about five calories, so even if I ate, yes, I said ate, not chewed, an entire pack, that pack of gum only came out to about fifty calories, and I often got sick way before I gained any weight.

I bought six to ten packs of gum A DAY, every day, and started chewing obsessively and robotically, swallowing every single stick of gum. This began my gateway to self-starvation and secrecy. For the next three years, almost all my meals consisted of sticks of gum, chewing and swallowing until I had lost over 30lbs.

Chewing gum was my way of satisfying my constant need to eat something. It also allowed me to satisfy the pressure of either losing weight or dealing with the harsh criticisms and judgment from those around me. I had to be obedient. Girls needed to be "good."

I had to lose the weight. I didn't care that what I was doing was unhealthy. I didn't care that the ten packs of gum a day could have potentially killed me. I just wanted to lose the weight, and chewing gum was my easy way out.

Shamefully Vanished
A Memoir of a Girl Out of Control

Like most mental disorders that develop in early adulthood, eating disorders usually begin during childhood, where parents either over-restrict their children's food intake or give them free reign to eat everything and anything they want while also calling them "fat" when they gain weight.

Family support systems are crucial when it comes to preventing the development of mental illnesses. Many overweight children hate the way they look mainly because of the reactions that other people have toward them, such as their physicians or family members, and as a result, they resort to hiding their food.

This creates shame and guilt in children, as they want to eat but cannot, as they want to please their families by losing weight but also feel the drive to satisfy their own needs. They usually resort to hiding and eating in privacy to avoid potential criticisms, hating themselves more for doing so, and eventually turn to food as their best friend.

Children are vulnerable and easily influenced by those close to them. Calling a child "fat" makes that child create new ways to hide the behaviors rather than actually changing them. Taking certain food away from children only makes them seek it out in other places rather than quelling their restrictions. Telling a child "no" often only fuels their desire to do it.

Shamefully Vanished
A Memoir of a Girl Out of Control

Shamefully Vanished
A Memoir of a Girl Out of Control

Chapter Four
My Anorexia Story

Although I heavily restricted my food intake as a child due to the fear of being called "fat" again, I never had an issue with body image until my freshman year at college. When I lost 30lbs, it was out of shame and guilt rather than out of vanity and self-hatred. I was terrified of being seen as a disappointment and being poked fun of just because I was a little overweight.

I cannot recall the exact sequence of events that led me to begin my year of self-starvation, but I do remember

Shamefully Vanished
A Memoir of a Girl Out of Control

loathing the body I was in and wanting to be someone else. About six months before my anorexia began, I started becoming antisocial. I locked myself in my dorm room for days at a time and refused to interact with anyone unless I absolutely had to.

I lost the friends I had made at the beginning of the school year because I kept making excuses to not join in on social events. I dropped out of all seven clubs I had signed up for and even began skipping classes. I just wanted to be left alone, causing me to fall deeper and deeper into a state of depression.

I remember becoming addicted to a TV sitcom about gymnastics, which featured a young woman who suffered from anorexia, and thinking to myself, "I wish I was her. I wish I was skinny. I wish I could lose ten pounds."

I admired everything about her: her looks, her personality, especially her weight, and I meticulously observed the techniques and excuses she used to avoid eating so I could imitate her.

Not once did I stop to reflect on whether my thoughts were logical. Not once did I question my own reasoning. At that time, my sole focus was to be skinny. My sole focus was to have this secret I could call my own and feel powerful by deceiving those around me.

To achieve this deluded perception of the body I thought I wanted, I limited myself to 500 calories a day, eating only two garlic and herb microwave pasta meals (at 250 calories each) and licking every last drop of sauce because I knew I would have to wait another 6-8 hours before I could eat my second one.

The first couple of weeks were easy. I was able to make it day after day without the desire to eat more than my allotted amount.

I kept a food diary of each day, neatly and obsessively documenting every nutritional fact that I was putting into my mouth. I refused to swallow a single crumb that was not part of my daily food intake, and if I did by accident, I immediately forced myself to work out for an hour to compensate.

I felt like I was in control of my own life. I felt powerful compared to others in that I was able to discipline myself and restrict my food intake while they could not. I distracted myself with movies and TV shows, and whenever I felt hungry and wanted to eat, I slept it off the pain.

However, soon I became more obsessive. My weight loss method through self-starvation alone developed a standstill, and I was even beginning to gain weight with water retention. I needed to do more. I was determined to lose those ten pounds despite the lengths I had to go through, and I refused to accept anything less.

I began exercising up to seven hours a day, every day, burning over 5,000 calories per workout, mostly on the elliptical because that is one of the quickest machines for burning calories as it combines both cardio and strength, while still maintaining my meager diet. Strenuous exercise

Shamefully Vanished
A Memoir of a Girl Out of Control

curbed my hunger pains, so the more my stomach growled, the harder I worked out.

Similar to my detailed food plan, I also documented every exercise I did, duration and calories burned included, in my journal, and I weighed myself every day, freaking out whenever I went up on the scale instead of down, despite whether it was water weight.

I eventually lost those ten pounds as I had initially wanted, but I did not stop. I wanted to lose more. It was as if something came over me and kept convincing me that ten pounds were not enough, and I needed to keep losing more weight or else I would become weak and a failure.

So, I continued. I continued my strict food and exercise plans daily for the next four months, but eventually had to stop because the school year was over, and I had to move back home with my parents for summer break.

I was anxious and petrified to go home because I had lost over twenty pounds within those past several months, and I knew going home meant my rigorous diet plan would be ruined. I feared that I would gain all the weight back because my mother would force me to eat meals outside my diet plan, and I wouldn't be able to work out every day as my privacy would become limited.

The first day I arrived at home, my mother became very concerned. She noticed how slim I had gotten and swore to herself that she would feed me until I gained the weight back. I panicked. I had spent all this time, all this effort, losing the weight, and now I would gain it all back?! I needed a plan, a plan to make my parents believe that I was eating when I actually wasn't.

I needed to pull out all the tricks I had learned from months of research, ranging from eating disorder documentaries to TV shows to online forums and, ironically, self-help books. I needed a disguise.

Shamefully Vanished
A Memoir of a Girl Out of Control

Shamefully Vanished
A Memoir of a Girl Out of Control

Chapter Five
Obsession and Failure

Since I had a full-time internship over the summer, working at a lab that required hours of standing and constant movement, I was able to use that as an excuse to regain some control of my diet, continue to exercise, and lie about eating.

My daily routine was as follows. I made it a goal to wake up early and walk at least 10,000 steps (never less, only more) before work. My joints started to become

Shamefully Vanished
A Memoir of a Girl Out of Control

fragile and weak, and I was no longer able to perform strenuous exercises as I weighed only 90lbs at that point.

Then I came home, drank straight black coffee (black coffee is supposed to suppress your appetite and speed up your metabolism), spent an hour eating one 15-calorie plain rice cake, and packed my lunch, which was always a large Tupperware consisting of plain iceberg lettuce. My mother always left before me in the mornings, and my father always slept in, so there was never anyone around to become suspicious what I was doing.

During lunch times at work, in order to avoid having to eat real food in front of people and in order to avoid going out to lunch with my coworkers, I either ate my lettuce and insisted it was a salad (since the lettuce made me feel full without all the added calories), or lied and said I was going to eat lunch at my uncle's and instead, walked around the city for an hour, always fabricating some sort of story about how "lunch at my uncle's" went in case anyone questioned me.

I had starved myself enough that I had begun training my stomach to stop growling. However, whenever it did, I suppressed the noise by either forcefully pressing my fist against my abdomen or punching my stomach a couple times, which were usually effective enough for several hours.

During dinners at home, I avoided having to eat by pretending to eat in my room, always with my bedroom door closed. I always received a large dinner plate from my mother, stacked high with fattening carbs. However, instead of eating at the dinner table like I was supposed

Shamefully Vanished
A Memoir of a Girl Out of Control

to, I insisted on bringing my meals into my bedroom every time, closing the door, blasting a song or a movie to mask what I was really up to, and instead of eating, I dumped my dinners into plastic bags I had stashed in my closet.

I hid the food-filled bags inside my closet, behinds piles of clothes to mask the smell, and brought the empty plates back out into the kitchen, pretending that I had eaten.

When I had liquid dinners such as soup, I poured them inside empty water bottles that I also had stashed in my closet. I then took both the bottles and the bags out of my closet every morning, shoved them inside my large tote bag, and threw them out in the trash cans at work before anyone discovered what I had been doing. Other times, I lied to my mother and said my boss took us all out to dinner, or that there was a social gathering and I had already eaten to avoid eating dinner at home.

I would purposely come home later, spending those extra hours walking, and pretended like I had eaten with my friends or coworkers. For months, I was never caught. I was losing more and more weight by the second and no one could figure out why.

I also became more obsessed with watching documentaries and reading forums on other people with eating disorders, anorexia, bulimia, and obesity all included. One of my favorite shows was "Supersize vs. Superskinny," a British reality show that swaps the meals of the overweight with the meals of the underweight.

Watching this show was like watching food pornography. I satisfied my desire to eat by pretending I

Shamefully Vanished
A Memoir of a Girl Out of Control

was eating the meals of the overweight, and I saw the underweight as "competition," either getting tips and tricks by watching their diets of twelve liters of Diet Coke a week and ten cups of coffee a day as appetite suppressants, or seeing what I could improve on and feeling strong when I weighed less than them. One dysfunctional thought that always ran through my head was, "The 'superskinny' looks overweight."

Paradoxically, I also became obsessed with another reality show called, "What's Eating You?," an American documentary following people with different types of eating disorders, ranging from bulimia to anorexia to pica (an eating disorder where people eat non-food like chalk and couch cushions rather than actual food). I didn't watch those shows for the education, as I liked to tell people; I watched those shows for ideas on how to "improve" my starvation methods.

One thing I noticed about the bulimics showcased when I watched this series was how they were both ashamed yet shameless about their binging and purging. They openly binged and purged in front of their family and in public, without a care about what others thought of them. Watching one woman eat mashed up cake from a garbage disposal and another woman throw up in bushes made me feel almost cringe worthy.

I didn't realize it at the time, but thinking back, that show was my first real exposure to the world of bulimia, and little did I know, those same acts that made me cringe became the acts that I began to also engage in.

Shamefully Vanished
A Memoir of a Girl Out of Control

I also became obsessed with Pro-Ana forums, an online community where those with eating disorders, mostly anorexics, come together and share ideas and thoughts on how to starve themselves, how to keep their secret by pretending to eat in front of others, and even ideas on how to harm themselves.

Eating disorders can take a massive toll on a person's psyche. The constant secrets and hiding when we know we need help make it a never-ending battle, driving us to loathe ourselves so much that we resort to self-harm and suicide. Because of this, hundreds of Pro-Ana forums have been taken down, but more only pop up in their place as the disease does not stop brainwashing sufferers.

***

One afternoon, while I was at work, I became famished. I was starving, starving like I had never starved before, and none of my methods to quell my hunger was working. This was the 184th day that I had continued my strict exercise and self-starvation routine, and my body began to eat away at itself. I needed to eat something. It was 4pm, and all I had eaten that day was a quarter of a rice cake and one leaf of lettuce.

Desperate, I left work, walked out to the closest convenience store near my job, bought a box of almond-flavored granola bars, and went back to work, promising myself that I was only going to eat one pack (which contained two bars) and eat nothing else for the rest of the night as that would be my "cheat meal."

Shamefully Vanished
A Memoir of a Girl Out of Control

I sat at my desk, opened the box, took one pack out, unwrapped it, broke the bars into pieces, and ate one. I could feel the intense sugar rush overpower me, and I couldn't remember the last time I had tasted something so delicious. The granola bar overwhelmed my taste buds so much to the point where I ate the entire pack within seconds, licking the wrapper and picking up every last crumb that had fallen onto my desk.

But I didn't stop, like I had told myself I would. I wanted more. Just "one" more. I told myself that 400 calories total for dinner wouldn't be too bad. I barely ate anything all day, and I can easily burn that off in no time by walking for a few hours after work. So, I ate another one. My taste buds became overwhelmed. I felt like I was in complete ecstasy. I felt that warm feeling inside of me, one which I haven't felt since I was a little girl.

The next thing I knew, all twelve packs of granola bars were inside my stomach, and I felt sick. I panicked. I had just devoured 2,400 calories in less than ten minutes, and I was terrified of gaining weight from it. I felt disgusted with myself because I had lost control of my diet and binged.

There was only one thought that pulsed through my head. I was not going to let this incident pass. I was not going to sleep it off and compensate for my mistake by resuming back to my diet the next day. Mistakes were not allowed. Making a mistake and ruining my diet plan meant I was a failure, a loser, a fake.

Shamefully Vanished
A Memoir of a Girl Out of Control

One error meant my entire life was over and that I might as well give up completely. One fault meant I would become my worst nightmare: a fat girl.

I had to get rid of all these calories despite what it took. Without thinking, I ran into the bathroom, slamming open the door, and locked myself in an empty stall. I attempted to stick my fingers down my throat to try and throw up the granola bars, only to end up gagging on my own saliva. I was not a purger at the time.

I had no idea what I was doing. The most I knew about purging was what I saw on my documentaries, and they all made it look so easy. I had never forced myself to throw up before that moment; it was only ever through nausea or illnesses.

Desperate, I ran back to the convenience store, bought a box of extra strength laxatives while avoiding eye contact with the cashier. He didn't know me, and he obviously didn't know what I was up to, but, still, I felt guilty. I felt like he was secretly judging me, realizing what I was up to as I bought both granola bars and laxatives within a span of less than an hour.

However, I couldn't reflect on my guilt too long as I had to remove this food from my body before I gained ten pounds from it.

I didn't even wait until I got back to work to swallow the pills. Immediately after leaving the store, I tore open the box while walking across the street, unconcerned with who was watching, and I downed eight pills at once (even though the recommended dosage was one), littering with my leftover trash in the process.

At that moment, I did not care about my dignity. I did not care about my appearance and trying to look "perfect" in front of people. At that moment, all I cared about was expelling the bars from my body.

I knew I looked like a mess, scurrying without looking up and mumbling to myself while twitching and fumbling with my fingers. My focus was no longer trying to achieve likability and acceptance by achieving the "perfect body" and being "in control." Instead, my focus had turned to praying that I still had enough time to shit all the calories from the granola bars out of me before they digested into fat.

I ran straight into the bathroom after swiping myself back into my work building. I locked myself in a stall and sat on the toilet. Nothing. I felt nothing. Not even the slightest tingle in my stomach as a sign that the pills were working. What a waste! What false advertising!

I took the rest of the pills from my pocket and chucked them into the trash can outside the stall, carefully covering them up with piles of paper towels to avoid someone else potentially seeing them and connecting them to me. I was pissed off. I had wasted over $15 on a box of laxatives that didn't even work, and now I was going to get fat from the granola bars.

Still disgusted and slightly nauseous, I went for a 4-hour walk after work around the dark streets of the glaring city, hoping to at least burn off some of the

Shamefully Vanished
A Memoir of a Girl Out of Control

unnecessarily added calories before going home, made an excuse to my mother that I didn't feel well, and climbed into bed in attempts to sleep off the nightmare of the day.

However, around 3am, my eyes widened, and I awoke when my stomach started to cramp. I felt like my intestines were being ripped out of my body, and I rolled off the bed and keeled over onto my carpet, thinking I was going to die. I ran into the bathroom and exploded on the toilet. I was in so much pain. I cried. I winced. I panicked as I struggled to breathe. I could not get a second's break from the intense pain I was experiencing and there was no sight of it ending soon.

I remained on the toilet seat for over five hours, crying and clutching my stomach, yelling and screaming in silence as I wretched in pain to try and avoid waking up the entire house. Ten flushes and a whole roll of toilet paper later, the pain had finally subsided. I cleaned myself and my surrounding area off, stepped onto my scale and was happily surprised that I had dropped five pounds almost instantly, despite the five hours of hell that I had just endured. I didn't care that all the weight dropped was probably due to water loss and dehydration. I was skinny, that was all that mattered.

I turned on my side and looked in my full-sized mirror, admiring my protruding hips and ribs as I rotated my body in various angles. I was in love. The fact that I almost died on the toilet did not completely register in my head. The memory of the moment I had spent agonizing in pain and crying in misery went right through my brain.

Shamefully Vanished
A Memoir of a Girl Out of Control

All I could focus on was how I "lost weight" and how the laxatives "worked as a diet supplement." Little did I realize, from that moment on, I would become addicted to supplements, unable to stop, always relying on the easy way out rather than self-control.

And so, my laxatives mayhem continued. Despite still attempting to stick to my strict low-calorie diet, I continued to rely on laxatives, falsely believing that they could help me lose even more weight. I began adding laxatives to my daily diet. I couldn't stand how the pills tasted when I tried them out the first time. That's when I discovered chocolate laxatives and began eating them like candy.

Every morning, I downed five pieces, using them to replace my breakfast hoping the laxatives would create some sort of opening in my intestines so whatever I put into my mouth would immediately flow out the other end. I confirmed this by counting chunks of apple skin in my stool each time to mentally try and piece together the whole fruit.

I had changed my diet from rice cakes and lettuce to apples. I ate three large apples a day, totaling 600 calories. The fiber from the apples either kept me full or made me cramp up, whichever came first (either way, it deterred me from wanting to eat more), and it was difficult to binge on apples as you can't just inhale them. That, plus the 150 calories of laxatives I ate per morning, made me shit like a rabbit every day during lunch. By the end of the summer, my weight had dropped down to 75lbs.

Shamefully Vanished
A Memoir of a Girl Out of Control

Chapter Six
Bulimia Begins

Back on campus during the fall semester of my second year in college, I tried to maintain my anorexic tendencies of living on a strict and meager diet while excessively exercising like I had successfully done during the spring before I left campus.

However, my willpower soon began to fade again. My binging session over the summer had created a gateway to more and more binging, to the point where I became

Shamefully Vanished
A Memoir of a Girl Out of Control

addicted and could not stop despite how hard I wanted to.

During my first week back, I found myself incessantly starving every minute of every day. Despite how hard I tried to stick to my diet of two microwavable meals a day, I still found myself constantly thinking about food, looking up images of food, and deliberately going out of my way so I could be around places that smelled like food.

By day three, I began to lose my anorexic habits, despite still calling myself "anorexic." Like many other anorexics, just that label itself made me feel powerful, as it is often known as the "cleanest of all eating disorders" and the one with the most "self-control."

On day three, my stomach growled voraciously while I was sitting in my Organic Chemistry class. To this day, I could not tell you what was taught during that lecture as all I could focus on was food and eating.

The hunger pains eventually became so strong that I was forced to go into the cafeteria and eat something. I chose a salad, hoping that a large bowl of romaine lettuce would be enough to fill my hunger cravings. It wasn't. I wanted more. I was still hungry. Since I had an unlimited meal plan, which, by the way, is deadly for someone with an eating disorder, I threw in the towel and gave in. I got back up and filled the biggest plate I could find with as much food as could fit on it.

People without eating disorders walk into a cafeteria, decide what they're in the mood for, carefully select the

Shamefully Vanished
A Memoir of a Girl Out of Control

best options, eat a small portion of said option, and go about their merry ways. People with eating disorders, like me, grab the first food in sight, inhale as much as they can at once without even registering what they have just put into their mouths, and go back for seconds, or thirds, or fourths, until they feel like they are about to explode.

By the end of the hour, I had eaten so much, from fried rice to chicken wings to burgers to cakes to waffles to everything in between, that I felt food beginning to travel back up my throat each time I burped. I felt food piled up to my chin, and my stomach became so bloated and stuffed that I could barely walk.

What have I done!? Guilt began to overwhelm me and anxiety began to creep in. I tried to quell the guilt by reasoning with myself that the binge session was a one-time event, and that it will never happen again. Everyone has binge days, right? It's called "cheat days." This binge can all be reversed and compensated if I just return to my diet plan tomorrow. One day won't kill me. I hope.

I opened my food diary and wrote in huge red letters "BINGE DAY. STARVE TOMORROW" on the calendar day, hoping that would be enough to motivate me. It did not work. Little did I know, I would never be able to go back to starvation mode again.

* * *

The next day, after I had told myself that I would resume back to my "normal" diet, I started off doing well. I had one apple for breakfast and went to class, but instead of going back to my room and studying as I had

Shamefully Vanished
A Memoir of a Girl Out of Control

planned, I made a sharp detour straight into the cafeteria for another binge session, telling myself that THIS would be the last time. I don't know what came over me. It was as if my mind had lost control of my body, and I was almost possessed to walk into the cafeteria and stuff my face.

Again, I ate and I ate until I could no longer move, and to make it worse, I repeated this pattern for the next five days, binging and binging until the brink of explosion, never figuring out how to resume my diet plan, and I eventually gave up. By the end of that week, I had gained eight pounds.

Unable to stop my binging habits, I became desperate. I was terrified that I had gained all that weight, with many more to come if I did not stop. I had to get rid of all this food and stop myself from gorging on everything I see, or I would become my worst nightmare: fat.

I ran into the nearest communal bathroom, right outside the cafeteria, and attempted to stick my fingers down my throat, once again, to try and vomit, but failed and instead, ended up gagging and choking on my own saliva. It seemed so easy on TV. Why couldn't I do it?

Panicking, I ran back to my dorm room, located on the third floor of the building, swung open my laptop and quickly scoured up ways to make myself throw up.

I came across a forum that mentioned how sometimes fingers can be too short to induce a gag reflex, suggesting sticking a toothbrush down the throat to trigger it instead. Desperate to try anything, I tried it. I grabbed my

Shamefully Vanished
A Memoir of a Girl Out of Control

toothbrush from my bathroom caddy, ran into the bathroom that I shared with my dorm mates, and violently shoved it down my throat.

I ended up gagging again, with only a small handful of food coming up. I tried it again, shoving the toothbrush deeper in, only to gag some more with viscous saliva pouring from my mouth instead of the food I had eaten.

I couldn't throw up. As much as I wanted to, my body refused to let me become bulimic. Since laxatives had helped me drop five pounds the last time I tried it, I assumed it would help again, despite still knowing that I was only losing water weight when I used the laxatives before.

I ran to the local grocery store, about 20-minutes from my dorm and in the middle of a dodgy and developing neighborhood, and bought their entire stock of chocolate laxatives, about thirty-five boxes, avoiding eye contact with the cashier as he rang me up, fully knowing that he was giving me a strange stare the entire time.

I ran back to my dorm room, made sure my roommate wasn't around, locked my door, and ate an entire box of chocolate laxatives in one sitting, all twenty-four pieces. After devouring an entire box, I sat on my bed and waited for the laxatives to take effect and pass the food I had devoured through me.

However, upon more research, I realized that I could not continue to rely on laxatives to pass the food through me and help me drop the pounds after my binges. Because I was losing so much water weight, I thought the laxatives were actually helping. Instead, I found out that I was only losing water weight but still gaining actual weight. The laxatives do not go into effect until the food had already been digested, hours after eating it.

Continuing to use them as my main diet option will only result in dehydration and an obese college student. I needed to find another solution. The laxatives could only be used as a supplement, not as a main diet option.

Shamefully Vanished
A Memoir of a Girl Out of Control

Shamefully Vanished
A Memoir of a Girl Out of Control

Chapter Seven
The Time I Almost Died

Over the course of the next two days, I continued with more research, refusing to go to class or even shower until I figured out a solution for my binging, and I tried out different methods I had found from the popular eating disorder forums that promoted Anorexia Nervosa.

One forum suggested dipping cotton balls (yes, actual cotton balls, not candy shaped like cotton balls) into orange juice (to mask the taste of you know, cotton!) and swallowing them whole as a way of obtaining the "fiber" needed without all the calories (wrong kind of fiber, but okay!).

The cotton balls were supposed to help me feel full without all the added calories from eating real food with digestible fiber. Despite realizing how insane this sounded, I was desperate enough to try it. People all over the Internet swore that it works, and I thought this would be my saving grace (and my easy way out).

I walked down to the local drug store, bought a bag of fluffy white cotton balls, and instead of dipping them into orange juice, as orange juice has too many calories, I dipped them into Diet Coke.

To my demise, I only ended up choking on the cotton balls. I broke down. I was so excited for this to work, but I could barely even swallow one as the fibers became entangled in my throat.

Next, I tried several infamous diets, ranging from the Cookie Diet to the Master Cleanse Diet to the Cabbage Soup Diet to the Baby Food Diet (yes, baby food). The Cookie Diet consists of eating a cookie (not just any cookie, you fat pig), but a special formulated cookie with high fiber content, for breakfast, lunch, and dinner for two days, which is supposed to curb your hunger (due to the fiber) and help you drop pounds since you're only technically taking in 450 calories a day.

Each cookie is supposedly 150 calories, with three grams of fiber and five grams of protein, and the diet is supposed to be done intermittently. I can personally vouch for this diet not working. Each cookie is as small as a poker chip, tastes disgusting, and does not curb the hunger pains whatsoever.

If anything, the dry chalk taste of the cookie would deter anyone from wanting to eat more than just one. But not me! I was still famished after my first cookie that I ended up eating the entire box in less than five minutes.

I then tried the Master Cleanse Diet, a detox diet that is supposed to last for three to ten days, where the only thing you are allowed to put into your mouth is a gag-worthy concoction made of lemon juice, maple syrup, cayenne pepper, and water.

The gist of this diet is that it's supposed to increase the amount of times you urinate per day, eventually causing you to piss out all your weight until you are at the point of passing out due to dehydration.

However, I couldn't even get past my first drink, as every time I brought it up to my nose, I felt nauseous. The next diet I tried is the 7-Day Cabbage Soup Diet, where you can only eat cabbages for an entire week. You are allowed to add other fruits and vegetables into the diet, but then you'll be back at square one with all the extra calories. This diet was dangerous.

I bought over a dozen heads of cabbage and made a delicious soup out of them, only to binge on six heads of cabbage in one day and had to force myself to throw out the rest as an attempt to stop additional binging. Plus, the cabbage made me really gassy!

Shamefully Vanished
A Memoir of a Girl Out of Control

The last nonsensical diet I tried was the Baby Food Diet, sworn to work by many famous celebrities. During the Baby Food Diet, you are only allowed to eat jars upon jars of baby food as meals rather than actual adult food.

Baby food is supposed to have all the necessary nutrients needed but a much lower caloric count than real food. This diet is mainly for people who cannot handle portion-control and like to steal jars of baby food away from actual babies. I'll be completely honest. Some of the baby food tasted pretty good; others tasted worse than baby puke itself, but all in all, they are just jars of mush.

Within a month, I had spent over $500 on gimmicky diet products, only to end up binging on them all. I then resorted to diet pills, such as Hydroxycut and Garcinia Cambogia, despite them costing over $60 a bottle. The diet pills contain an extract that was supposed to help suppress my appetite while burning off fat at the same time.

However, I learned the hard way that diet pills are not for everyone, and especially not when taken on an empty stomach as I swallowed two whole Hydroxycut Extra Strength pills one early morning.

Later that night, I woke up around 2am with what felt like a heart attack. I expected some side effects from the diet pills, as with any medication, but not to extent that I experienced. I rolled off my bed and began gasping for air on the floor, screaming out in pain for someone to call an ambulance.

Shamefully Vanished
A Memoir of a Girl Out of Control

Unfortunately, just my luck, all my dorm mates were out the night I actually needed them around. No one heard me, and I was left curled up on my dusty dorm room carpet feeling like I was about to die.

After two hours of unbearable pain, I struggled for my mini trash can, threw up in it, swore I could see blood mixed in with the concoction, and fell asleep, still curled up on the floor with my trash can filled with vomit lying beside my head.

***

I woke up (miraculously) the next morning feeling much better. However, I did not want to experience another moment like I had last night ever again and flushed every single pill I had remaining to avoid the temptation of taking them again. $200 down the toilet but all I could focus on was what diet plan I could try next. The Gum Diet (aka, the diet where you only eat, yes, eat as in swallow, not just chew, packs and packs of gum every day) had worked for me in middle school, helping me lose fifteen pounds.

I had hoped that the Gum Diet would work for me again this time around. I had hoped that the premise of having gum stick to my esophagus would prevent me from wanting to eat. However, I forgot to take into account that I had not begun serial binging yet during my gum-chewing days in middle school. All the binging I had been exposed to so quickly made it almost impossible to stick to any sort of diet without resorting to inhaling everything in sight.

Shamefully Vanished
A Memoir of a Girl Out of Control

The last diet option I tried in order to counterattack my binging habits was chugging ipecac. Ipecac is a chemical substance that people ingest to help stimulate vomiting when they accidentally swallow poison. Ipecac is highly toxic, and if taken in large doses, can be fatal. However, the idea of gaining weight continued to frighten me more than the idea of death, so I tried it anyway, hoping ipecac would be my saving grace where I could have my cake and eat it too.

I know what you're probably thinking. I'm expending all this effort and risking my life just to expel food from my body when there are billions of people in the world dying from the lack of food. Save the pity party. I know. We all know, but eating disorders are about more than just common sense and acts that people think we can control.

Anyway, back to my story. Since I didn't have a car at the time, I had to take a sketchy bus in the middle of nowhere to a store about 25-miles north just to buy ipecac. Because ipecac is so toxic, many stores do not stock them for the fear of it getting into the hands of the wrong person (i.e., me).

The stores that do stock them keep them under lock and key for special cases only, with one store manager believing me when I told him I am a single mother with a 3-year-old child at home who just swallowed rat poison. Lying becomes almost second nature when you're desperate.

I was too excited to test the "miracle work," as some forums called it, of ipecac. I didn't even wait until I got back to my dorm. A little over half the trip back, I got off the bus when I spotted a local fast-food restaurant known for their dirt-cheap but super greasy and super unhealthy meals. I didn't care. I had the intention of throwing everything back up anyway, so what did I care? I walked into the restaurant and ordered close to half their menu, with a total cost of $120, receiving over twenty large bags of take-out.

Despite insisting over six times that all this food was for a party, there's something about a small girl buying her weight in food that always seem to welcome strange and judgmental stares, despite the reason. The workers didn't know the real reason I was buying all this food; they didn't need to know.

With my head down, I timidly said "thank you" as I struggled to grab all the bags, insisting I was fine when they offered to help me carry them out to "my car" which, of course, didn't exist, and we would just end up standing outside with thirty pounds of fast food.

Wobbling out of the restaurant, I continued to walk several blocks south until I spotted a strip mall with a grocery store, several small restaurants and bars, a few clothing stores, and a bank. Strip malls were easy binge locations as there are so many people that it makes it that much harder to get caught.

Still lugging my weight in burgers and fries, I trudged behind the grocery store and found a row of dumpsters lining the back parking lot, which was only used for loading trucks and employees, so it was usually empty and quiet. I crouched behind the dumpsters, trying hard

Shamefully Vanished
A Memoir of a Girl Out of Control

to ignore the stench, and quickly ate my burgers, one by one, washing them down with fries dipped in milkshakes.

After devouring all $120 worth of food (to this day, I still don't know how I managed to fit all that food inside my stomach in one go), I was barely able to stand up. Have you ever eaten so much that your stomach expanded a foot past your chest, where you feel so heavy in your abdomen that you're about to fall over? I felt so disgusting that I couldn't even fit one more fry into my mouth.

Rummaging through my mountain of wrappers, cartons, and cups, I found my bottle of ipecac. I broke the seal of the cap and sniffed the content. It was rancid! The scent of ipecac is the same as the scent you experience when you mix five different cleaners together to clean an overly abused toilet. Still, I held my nose and chugged, until I drank over half the bottle. The MAXIMUM safe dosage for ipecac is one tablespoon, not half the bottle!

Regardless, the ipecac sure was effective as I did vomit. However, rather than having half-digested food come back up like I had hoped, I felt my throat begin to burn as I saw stomach acid and blood spew out of my mouth and straight onto a dumpster. I felt nauseous.

The ipecac not only burned through the food that were in my stomach, but it also burned through my intestines, and I was sporadically coughing up blood. I lied, curled up in a fetal position, on the ground for hours, secretly resentful that no one had stopped by to save me from myself.

Shamefully Vanished
A Memoir of a Girl Out of Control

Finally, when I was able to regain my energy again, I poured the rest of the ipecac bottle down the sewer, swearing to myself that I would never go near ipecac again, despite how desperate I was.

Shamefully Vanished
A Memoir of a Girl Out of Control

Chapter Eight
To Vomit or Not to Vomit?

Still, I refused to give up on my quest for the perfect method I could use to continue my binging habits, and I sure as hell wasn't going to just let the food sit inside me and translate into obesity. What kind of self-control would I have then? Starvation was no longer an option. I had given up on that long ago, with no way of obtaining it back.

Clearly, I had no self-control. I couldn't even succeed at being an anorexic. Fat pig. Why even bother anymore?

Shamefully Vanished
A Memoir of a Girl Out of Control

What's the point? I'm just a fat cow who will remain fat forever. Unless.

After the ipecac made me vomit up my organs, I went back to "the toothbrush method," the last hope I had that wasn't going to send me to my grave…yet. However, this time, I was determined to make myself throw up more than only a handful of food mixed in with a gallon of saliva. Binge after binge, I continued to shove a toothbrush down my throat to try and induce vomiting over the course of the next two months. By that point, I had gained nearly twenty pounds, and I was beginning to become more and more depressed and out of control by the second.

Just when I was about to give up, a miracle, or rather a gateway to my own self-destruction, arose. Eventually, all the constant pressure that I was forcing against my throat loosened my gag reflexes and made it easier for me to throw up.

More food came up rather than just spit and saliva, and by month three, I had successfully achieved the "hands-free purge," a purging technique that is a godsend for most bulimics because it literally means that all that is required is a simple bend-over and a gentle push against the abdomen to watch about 85% of the contents come back up, only requiring one or two more to remove the remaining.

Looking back, this "great achievement" that I was so proud of accomplishing, only proved to be my worst nightmare. When I was using a toothbrush, it was a chore every single time. The amount of effort it took to

Shamefully Vanished
A Memoir of a Girl Out of Control

overcome the pain of shoving a foreign object down my throat and leaving it there in attempts to try and force myself to choke was enough to make me want to quit a few times.

With the "hands-free" method, having to stick anything down my throat was completely out of the equation. This method made throwing up almost too easy, to the point where I began to feel guilty if I didn't expel everything that went inside my body, water included. Then the nightmare began.

I started off my bulimic episodes fairly lightly. During the daytime, I would try and eat like a "normal" person, limiting my calories during the day while only binging during the evenings. In the evenings, I allowed myself to eat anything and everything I could and then forced myself to throw it all up.

Not long after, however, the episodes became worse. I went from eating light in the mornings to not eating at all, and then binging on even more than my usual during the nights because, by that point, I was starving from depriving myself all day of food.

Soon, I found myself binging and purging all day, every day, skipping classes and work just to spend hours at the cafeteria every morning, stuffing my face with everything from powdered eggs to waffles drenched in syrup to cereal both with and without milk to just plain oats even though I found them disgusting.

My binges started off with items that looked appetizing, food that I constantly craved and had been depriving myself of during my starvation period. However, as anyone who has ever truly binged would agree, there is never enough food until our stomachs feel about the size of a hot air balloon, and we have long passed the walk of shame down the buffet aisle.

Running out of food is never the solution to stop eating; running out of space is what forces us to stop. A true binge has no limits when the hunger pains are still there. We will eat everything in sight, as unappetizing as they are, until we have satisfied the craving to continue eating.

After inhaling everything I could fit inside my stomach, I snagged a few breakfast sandwiches on my way out the door, shoved them inside my bag, and walked into the communal bathroom adjacent to the cafeteria to throw up.

I then proceeded up to my dorm room so I could polish off my breakfast sandwiches while my dorm mates were all in class. I also pulled out my junk food stash from my hidden suitcase underneath my bed, filled with expired chips and cookies I had bought from the Dollar Store, and piled those on top of the breakfast sandwiches that were already fast inside my stomach. I have learned during my binging sessions that mixing junk food (aka, food that could easily break apart) in with "normal" food usually results in an easier purge.

I threw up the breakfast sandwiches and junk food in the toilet my dorm mates and I shared, disregarding the fact that toilet water splashed back onto my face in the process, and headed back downstairs to the cafeteria for

Shamefully Vanished
A Memoir of a Girl Out of Control

my lunch-time binge. Having a cafeteria on the bottom floor of my dorm building was dangerous. It made binging that much more accessible, even when I no longer had the will to purge.

Returning only just two hours after I had already been there for breakfast, I was worried that the cafeteria workers would recognize me and question why I was coming back so soon after having stuffed my face at breakfast. Because of that fear, I walked into the cafeteria with my hood up and a scarf wrapped around my face in attempts to mask who I was in case anyone recognized me.

During lunch, I did the same thing, eating as much as I could in one sitting while smuggling a bag full of sandwiches and cookies back to my dorm so I could continue to binge in my room. A few hours later, I went back down to the cafeteria during dinnertime and repeated the entire process until I passed out shortly after my last purge, preparing myself to restart the cycle the next morning.

As my binges increased, so did my appetite, and soon, my stomach began to expand. It had gotten to the point where even going to the cafeteria three times a day and smuggling over twenty sandwiches out per meal time were not enough. I began to feel hungry during early mornings and late nights when all the cafeterias on campus were closed. I resorted to ordering multiple boxes of pizzas at once and enough Chinese food to feed 15+ every night to try and quell my off-hour cravings.
I refused to sleep.

Shamefully Vanished
A Memoir of a Girl Out of Control

There was never enough time for it. Eating became my top priority. I ordered delivery when my dorm mates weren't around and hid them under my bed until they went to sleep. Then I would bring my delivered meals outside my room and binge on them in the common hall, purging in the lobby toilet at 4am when no one was around.

Still, I always made sure to line the toilet bowl with piles of toilet paper to prevent any splash back and sound proof the noise in case anyone did happen to walk by during the early hours.

I also learned to suppress my gagging and coughing when it comes to vomiting. Still, sometimes they slip out when large chunks of digested food attempted to force its way up due to a lack of liquids to soften the solids, or if I drank too many carbonated drinks such as soda, which caused me to reflexively burp or gag due to too much gas.

To finish it off, I would then eat between 10-15 chocolate laxatives every night to remove any calories that I was not able to throw up. Sometimes, the stores would run out of laxatives, regular and chocolate included, and I had to resort to suppositories to induce expulsion, which is just as awkward and embarrassing as you think.

I also pretended to have parties while ordering or buying masses of food at once, as well as ordering or buying my "fixings" from different locations, sometimes even having to travel further away to avoid suspicions and running into people I knew. I dumped out all the empty containers and boxes in the large dumpsters

Shamefully Vanished
A Memoir of a Girl Out of Control

behind my dorm building rather than in my hallway trash cans to disperse the blame to more people if anyone were to ever find out what I had been doing.

I began running out of money each day, and some days, I resorted to binging and purging on expired food, my own vomit, and even stolen food from my dorm mates. I was desperate. I was willing to do anything I could, even illegally, to get my hands on anything I could shove inside my mouth.

I even got a part-time job at a local coffee shop to make some extra money for my binging habits. Bonus, working at a coffee shop meant I had free access to leftover pastries and bagels, which I always grabbed and finished binging on before going back to my dorm, only one block away from my job, throwing them up in the lobby bathroom on the way up.

Shamefully Vanished
A Memoir of a Girl Out of Control

Chapter Nine
Why Did I Confess?

I wish I had never started vomiting in the bath tub. Gross, right? I know. It was never something I thought I would ever be desperate enough to do, but once I started, it became extremely difficult to stop. Throwing up in the bath tub meant it was a lot easier to clean, and turning on the water added an additional level of noise I could use to cover my tracks.

Flushing the toilet fifteen times every time I went inside to "pee," was beginning to seem suspicious to my dorm

Shamefully Vanished
A Memoir of a Girl Out of Control

mates. The bath tub became my go-to purging spot for almost three months before I finally clogged the drain after trying to wash down three pizzas worth of vomit at once. Clogging the drain and seeing all my food come back up was petrifying.

For bulimics, the satisfaction comes from seeing how much food we are able to EXPEL from our bodies and watching it all wash AWAY, cleansing ourselves from the guilt and shame. Watching it all just sit there makes us come face to face with our inner demons.

However, seeing everything I had thrown up come back up also felt like my wake-up call to finally put an end to this bulimic cycle I was trapped in. I became frantic and anxious that I was surely going to get caught because I had no way of getting this vomit to go down the drain. I kept picturing the shameful conversation I would have with my dorm mates when they walked in on me sitting on the bathroom tiles next to a bath tub filled with two feet of vomit.

I even reached my hand down the drain to try and clear away the contents, but it didn't work. Fucked. I was fucked. Ready to throw in the towel, I typed up an email to my Psychology professor, asking him if I could set up a meeting at his earliest convenience, fully ready to disclose my secret. As soon as I hit "send," my vomit-infused water began draining, saving me...two seconds too late as my professor emailed me back telling me to see him in his office in an hour. Fuck.

***

Shamefully Vanished
A Memoir of a Girl Out of Control

I guess part of me wanted my secret to become exposed. My bulimic episodes began as a sense of regaining control of my body after I could not stop binging.

Somewhere down the line, it began taking control over me as my days, 24/7, began revolving around my disease rather than around living my life. I had skipped so many classes that I was on the brink of failing, and I had spent so much money, so quickly, that my bank began to question fraud. Part of me needed a way out, but the other part of me still needed something that I could call "mine."

I could have very well canceled that meeting or just not show up and dealt with the awkwardness during class the next week. I could also have lied and talked about something else, something class related, instead of exposing myself. But I didn't. I told him the truth, which I now regret doing, but at the time, it felt like my only chance at saving myself from myself.

I told him everything, from when I developed anorexia to my binging and extreme diet cycles to my now bulimic episodes. He was shocked, just as I had feared. He began putting the pieces together as to why I had been so instinctual in my papers and assignments on eating disorders and mental health dysfunction...because I had been personally living in them.

He encouraged me to visit the counseling center and speak to a therapist. Encouraged, not forced. I could have very well skipped out on going and pretended like I went. I could have also lied again and told the counselors

Shamefully Vanished
A Memoir of a Girl Out of Control

something other than what I actually told them: a lie, but a lie that changed my life forever.

For those of you who have been to therapy, therapists are extremely well-trained at making you confess your secrets, that sometimes, you end up confessing to things that aren't even true. Sure, I told my counselor about my anorexia. Hell, I even told my counselor about my bulimia, the full unfiltered story.

But for some reason, I also told my counselor that I was suicidal, that I walked the streets at night hoping I would get shot, an action and thought that never crossed my mind, but I proceeded with the lie anyway, digging myself into a deeper hole.

Because I made myself sound suicidal when I wasn't actually, I was put on a forced medical leave from school the very next day, and I wasn't allowed to return until I had both my eating disorder and my suicidal thoughts under control, and by that, I mean under the school's control.

After paying thousands of dollars in tuition, I was forced to leave school until the dean deemed I was physically and mentally fit enough to return. It's a college campus. There were probably hundreds of other students just like me, and I was the only one foolish enough to turn myself in, watching all my hopes and dreams get flushed down the toilet.

Shamefully Vanished
A Memoir of a Girl Out of Control

Shamefully Vanished
A Memoir of a Girl Out of Control

Chapter Ten
Kicked Out and Broke

Before I left campus, both the counseling center and the dean worked together to organize a spot for me at an inpatient clinic for those suffering from severe eating disorders so they could be sure that I'd go. They also needed a note from the clinic that I was in optimal mental and physical shape before I was allowed back in school. Otherwise, I would continue to perish in my own destruction.

Shamefully Vanished
A Memoir of a Girl Out of Control

However, my admission at the clinic wasn't scheduled to start until two months after I was forced to leave school, forcing me to move back home with my parents, my parents who still, to this day, refused to believe that I had a problem.

So, they left me alone, for most of the days at least. Going home felt like a kick in the face. I had worked so hard to get into a great school, only to end up back home less than two years later. I was disappointed in myself. How did I let it get so bad, going from simply holding onto a secret to getting kicked out of school? I hated my college for forcing me to leave, and I hated myself for telling the truth instead of continuing to hide.

I didn't have depressed thoughts when I first left school. However, that all changed when my freedom and education were taken away from me. The more I reminisced on getting kicked out of school, the more depressed I became. The more depressed I became from having moved back home, the more I continued my bulimic tendencies to ease the pain and create a distraction.

My binging and purging habits became much worse when I moved home. I no longer had to be paranoid of my dorm mates catching me in the act, allowing me to spread out all my food and admire them before they were all thrown up.

It also didn't help that there was a supermarket less than half a block from me, with a self-checkout line that allowed me to come and go as I pleased without having to deal with awkward "Weren't you just here?"

Shamefully Vanished
A Memoir of a Girl Out of Control

conversations. Because I was living at home and had a set chunk of time when my parents were out of the house, my binging and purging cycles went from ten times a day to over thirty.

I ate everything: cookies, cakes, pies, chips, crackers, ice cream, donuts, mac and cheese, hot dogs, ramen noodles, canned soups, microwave meals, pasta dinners, basically everything I could get my hands on either inside the house or at the grocery store. I also walked to nearby convenience stores and fast-food restaurants when I craved hot meals, buying hundreds of dollars' worth of burgers and fries, pizzas, and subs.

Running out of food never stopped me. Whenever I ran out but still felt the craving, I resorted to binging on whatever I found inside my parents' cabinets: expired canned beans, oatmeal that were just over four years old, stale and moldy bread, and even powdered creamer, which when mixed with water, tasted like custard. I went on an eating frenzy. My bulimia got worse with all the free time I had because I no longer had to worry about failing all my classes if I didn't stop eating and start studying.

* * *

One day, my mother found my food trash in the garbage bin. I had tried to bury them all underneath the rest of the trash, but she had suspiciously dug through the disgusting garbage and found my stash. She was catching on. I had to get more creative. I couldn't risk getting caught again. If I didn't have binging and purging, I had nothing.

Shamefully Vanished
A Memoir of a Girl Out of Control

I began hiding my food trash in my suitcases, in between old textbooks, underneath my mattress, and even threw bags of trash over the backyard fence and onto the street behind the house. One time, I tried throwing out two garbage-sized bags of trash in the dumpster behind the supermarket, only to get caught, so I left those bags in my neighbor's backyard instead. After a month of living at home and not having a stream of income, my bank account had gone down to negative $250.

That should have been my wake-up call to stop, but instead, I began stealing, first from my parent's stash of cash they had hidden to dumpster diving behind restaurants and eating whatever I could find that resembled food to stealing from supermarkets and convenience stores by unwrapping packages and shoving the contents inside my pockets or my mouth when no one was looking. I knew where all the cameras were, and I knew exactly how to avoid getting caught.

My dinners at home eventually became supervised as I began losing more weight. No longer did I have the freedom to "eat" in my bedroom as my mother became apprehensive of what I had been doing. Every night, in order to "fatten me up," my dinners were over 2,000 calories each and full of carbs and fats.

Terrified of letting even ten calories linger inside my body, I developed new ways to purge at home, even with my parents inside the house, including purging in the toilet while pretending to take a shower, purging in a plastic bag in my room, purging in the bushes outside while pretending to take a casual stroll around the block,

Shamefully Vanished
A Memoir of a Girl Out of Control

and purging in the garbage disposal when my mother was in the shower.

My parents could not figure out how I was still losing weight even after watching me eat in front of them. They took me to a medical physician in attempts to try and "fix" me, but the physician was completely ignorant when it came to mental illnesses and eating disorders.

Like most medical doctors (plus it didn't help that he was from the Eastern part of the world where mental disorders are less common), this doctor had not been educated on eating disorders, still viewing them as "diet choices" and "quick fixes" rather than anything serious.

His solution for my parents was for me to eat an entire jar of mayonnaise so I could gain quick and easy weight. He, like my parents, thought I had full control over what I was doing and simply yelled at me to stop, calling me selfish for stealing my parents' lives away from them.

Shamefully Vanished
A Memoir of a Girl Out of Control

Shamefully Vanished
A Memoir of a Girl Out of Control

Chapter Eleven
First Residential Experience

The day finally arrived. The day of my supposedly hopeful redemption. Walking into the residential clinic was like walking into a nursing home. Everyone was fragile. Some were hooked onto feeding tubes. Others had to walk around with crutches or sit in wheelchairs because their osteoporosis had caused their bones to become too weak to support them.

The only difference was, every patient in the clinic was young. The average age of the patients there was only 22 and comprised of all women, many of whom looked twice their age as the lack of nutrition had damaged their youthful skin.

My parents had hoped that this would be the wake-up call that I needed, but instead, like it was for most of the residents there, staying in this clinic became a competition. There was an unspoken opposition among all the eating disorder patients there, especially the anorexics, on who could be the skinniest and who could hide their food the most.

I learned tricks I didn't even know about at the clinic, such as hiding food in certain places inside my mouth just to spit it out later, hiding food inside my fingernails, hiding food inside my underwear when no one was looking, and refusing to eat so I would be given a liquid supplement instead, which was easier to purge without the risk of getting caught.

Day one. 4am. Every morning, everyone woke up before sunrise to get weighed by the overweight nurses who gave us judgmental eyes while we wore nothing but a thin gown and our underwear. Trudging sleepily and weakly down a dark and thin carpeted hallway, we all got patted down like prisoners to make sure that we were not hiding anything in our underwear that would increase our weights on the scale.

We all had "goal weights" that we needed to hit before we were allowed to get discharged. "Goal weights" were weights that the counselors and nurses deemed "physically functional" based on our heights. However, the more "physically functional" we became, the more "mentally dysfunctional" we also became.

Shamefully Vanished
A Memoir of a Girl Out of Control

I needed to gain twenty pounds in order to hit my goal weight, a weight I have not been at in over three years. Also, if our electrolytes were low, we had to drink Gatorade (not even the low-calorie version), adding to our caloric intake but not counting as part of our daily meal plans.

I was diagnosed as "Anorexic with a Binge-Purge Subtype," which meant that even though I purged, I was still severely underweight enough to be classified as an anorexic. To be categorized as a bulimic, I would have had to be at a normal BMI or be overweight.

I was proud of my label. The anorexics were considered the "clean" ones among those with eating disorders. I was proud of myself for receiving the label that meant I still had control over my body. It also meant I was able to eat what I wanted and remain super skinny. Clearly, I had a fucked-up mindset.

Meal times were based on levels. All new patients started at the bottom level and were given set meal plans that could not be deviated from, meals of about 1,500 calories each for breakfast, lunch, and dinner, and had to sit at the dining table and eat the entire meal, every crumb and every drop under supervision, before being allowed to leave. If we didn't finish before the allotted 30-minute time frame was over, we would get two liquid supplement drinks to make up the calories of the food.

On the next level, we were given the choice to choose what we wanted to eat, but the portions were still decided for us because they still didn't trust us enough to not abuse the freedom.

Shamefully Vanished
A Memoir of a Girl Out of Control

The third and highest level was complete freedom, what everyone strived for. We were able to control our own portions and the counselors trusted that we were going to finish our meals.

Liquid supplements were rarely given out on level three because residents either portioned less than what they were supposed to for themselves, or they bucked up and ate their meals like normal human beings.

Supplements were only ever given out to those at this level when they either flat-out refused to eat or when they couldn't finish their meals in time due to other psychological issues.

I ate the same thing every day. Change was scary. Breakfast consisted of plain yogurt with Cheerios, a fruit cup, and orange juice. We weren't allowed to have coffee until level three because many residents still used coffee to boost their metabolisms and burn more calories.

Lunch was usually some kind of undercooked burger or meatloaf, and dinner almost always had potatoes or something equally full of carbohydrates. Potatoes are the worst food for people with eating disorders. They are heavy, full of carbs and they make you bloated and sick.

During the day, we had individual therapy with our counselors as well as different types of group therapies that our counselors assigned to us based on what THEY thought we needed. The group therapies ranged from art to music to CBT (Cognitive Behavioral Therapy) to role-playing family behaviors, but really, they were all just in place for patients to bullshit their way toward discharge.

Shamefully Vanished
A Memoir of a Girl Out of Control

We received notes in our mailboxes of the therapy sessions we needed to go to along with meal plan options for those on level two. We also met with a psychiatrist once a week who prescribed us medications, medications that almost never worked.

If we didn't show up to a group session or a therapy session, the counselors docked us points, an excuse to keep us in there longer or until our insurance companies stop covering our stays and the clinic is forced to kick us out.

During the evenings, we did "social activities," such as watched movies or had karaoke and knitting nights. Every girl inside the clinic became experts at either knitting or crocheting, despite having experience beforehand or not. It was the only way to pass time without dying of boredom, plus we all needed something to keep our anxiety at bay.

At the end of each week, we all collectively made over 350 scarves and hats. During my first week, I shared a room with a 60-year-old obese smoker whom I found repulsive and didn't want to be around. So, I made up a lie and told the counselors I needed to be moved because I couldn't physically breathe around her because of the cigarette smoke, when in truth, I just found her disgusting and fat. Shallow? I know. Let's move on.

During my third week, a group of the patients took a trip to a grocery store with some of the counselors. The purpose of this trip was to treat ourselves to something small, which we had to buy with our own money, and choose out a dessert or snack that wasn't low-calorie or low-sugar, which we also had to buy with our own money. We then had to eat the dessert or snack in front of everyone at the clinic, fully knowing they would judge us or call us "fat" in private.

The trick was to pick the dessert or snack item with JUST ENOUGH calories and fat to "pass the test," such as protein bars or granola. However, I panicked and ended up choosing a high-calorie dessert that my bulimic side craved, a dessert the other residents called "brave."

Eating our dessert or snack item in front of all the other residents was supposed to help us become more comfortable with being surrounded by "trigger food" and feel okay eating them, while also knowing that we would not become gargantuan as a result. "Trigger food" were food that would normally cause anorexics to starve or over-exercise and bulimics and overeaters to binge.

The trip to the grocery store freaked out the anorexics. Their anxiety shot up from being surrounded by aisles upon aisles of food. I bought a chocolate cake because I thought I would be able to purge it up later. However, I was only allowed to eat half of it, which quickly burned through my stomach acid so nothing came up during my purge attempt, causing me to digest a shit ton of calories.

Some of the residents also went on a trip to a clothing store, but I wasn't allowed to go because my therapist said I didn't have Body Dysmorphic Disorder. Fuck her.

Shamefully Vanished
A Memoir of a Girl Out of Control

Shamefully Vanished
A Memoir of a Girl Out of Control

Chapter Twelve
Getting Worse

After four weeks of residential boredom, I was finally discharged, not because I had gained the weight I needed, but because my insurance had run out and my parents were forced to take me home. I wasn't suicidal before I left campus nor was I suicidal when I walked into the inpatient residential eating disorder clinic and was forced to relinquish control.

However, because I was discharged without consent from my therapist that I was "cured," I was still denied

Shamefully Vanished
A Memoir of a Girl Out of Control

from going back to school. The dean specifically specified that I needed full approval from my therapist stating that I was mentally stable before I was allowed back on campus, as I slowly watched the costly tuition I had paid go down the drain.

Before I left the clinic, I received a bottle of Prozac from my psychiatrist to take daily in order to suppress my depressive thoughts and, hopefully, ease my bulimic habits as Prozac is supposed to also act as a hunger suppressant.

Unfortunately, within ten hours of moving back home, my bulimic habits started up again and, once again, I began binging and purging on everything I could find (despite feeling guilty for wasting my parents' money on treatment). However, because my parents started to catch on, I had to develop more clever ways to hide my habits.

I made up a job that I told my parents I had to go to every day, and instead of going to said job, I hopped onto buses instead to hit up different buffets around town. Buffets are a dream for bulimics, especially for bulimics without money. All you need to do is find the ones where you pay AFTER you are done eating because then, you can just sneak out without anyone noticing.

However, the trick is to hit up different buffets each time so no one recognizes you, and you never get caught. Lucky for me, there were over 200 buffets near where I lived, so by the time I started repeating them, they had already forgotten about me. I was broke. I did not have a single dime to my name. However, I had stolen before I

Shamefully Vanished
A Memoir of a Girl Out of Control

went into residential, and therefore, had no problem stealing again.

***

I remember one particular buffet binge, like many others, where I started off light, eating something I could live with if the food were digested, something to line my stomach, like oatmeal, which takes longer to digest so everything else I ate afterward wouldn't burn straight through and convert into added pounds.

After being shown to my table and ordering a glass of iced water, I got up from my seat and sprang into action. I started off small and light, as I had planned. I grabbed a medium-sized bowl and filled it up with oatmeal, quickly eating it so I could grab more food.

After my bowl of oatmeal, I went for the good stuff. It was game time. I started with breakfast food, devouring waffles, eggs, cereal, pancakes, hash browns, and tater tots, eating up to four large plates until they brought out lunch items. I excused myself to puke in the bathroom so I could empty my stomach and fill up on lunch.

Lunch was usually the same: noodles, fried rice, fried chicken, fries, burgers, and about ten donuts, all washed down with fresh hot soup and melted ice cream to soften the food and make them easier to purge.

After stuffing my face with six large plates from lunch, I pocketed about thirty cookies, made sure the coast was clear, pretended to use the bathroom, and instead, bolted out the back door when no one was looking, throwing up what I had just eaten behind the dumpster of the buffet restaurant.

I was always careful to look for security cameras before throwing up in public. It wasn't the public act of violation that scared me; it was the shame of people knowing that I threw up in public.

Because I had just thrown everything from the buffet back up, I became hungry again on the way home. I got off the bus when I saw a Dollar Store and stole over $20 worth of junk food.

By that point, I had become a pro at scanning out all the hidden cameras, and I knew exactly where I needed to hide to avoid getting caught, despite each store having a different setup.

I wore jackets and sweatshirts that were three sizes too big for me so I could stuff the stolen food inside them while walking out, pretending like I was just another casual browser. I then found alleys or parks with overgrown trees, opened all my goodies, and ate them all within 20-minutes. Since junk food were easy to purge, and they also dispersed between solid food, I usually end my binges with junk food so I could also bring up anything I had not purged during my other sessions.

I finished the last bite of cookie, hid the trash behind some trees, and purged in an isolated area, whether that was a dirty alleyway or behind a park bench. I couldn't stand walking down the alleys. They always reeked of cocaine and prostitution, contained shit from one or fifty people, and were usually enough to make me black out from the stench. Still, alleys were the easiest places to hide, so I continued using them.

This chaotic cycle continued over the next two months, until one day, for some reason, I felt really depressed about my life and how I was wasting it. I had gone from being at the top of my class and voted "most likely to succeed" to throwing up behind dumpsters, getting kicked out of school, and going bankrupt. I became suicidal, and I wanted this nightmare of a life to end.

Lying in bed one afternoon, I opened my bottle of Prozac, and I downed all forty pills at once, hoping that the overdose would put me out of my misery as I fell asleep.

However, rather than not waking up ever again, I woke up to my mother screaming and my brother frantically calling an ambulance. I had not died from the overdose and, instead, had gotten myself into deeper shit. Once again, I was taken to inpatient, this time in a psychiatric hospital.

Shamefully Vanished
A Memoir of a Girl Out of Control

Chapter Thirteen
I Watched Someone Die

Inpatient psychiatric hospitals are a lot different from residential clinics. In eating disorder residential clinics, they focus on helping you get healthy, both physically and mentally. They take the time to check in with you, weigh you, understand you, and make sure your health is at an optimal minimum before releasing you back into the wild, unless your insurance runs out like mine did.

Eating disorder residential clinics are welcoming, warming, and safe places to meet new friends. Inpatient psychiatric hospitals are the complete opposite. Dark. Scary. Lonely.

Patients treated like guinea pigs. In inpatient psychiatric hospitals, they use a "get in, get out" method, where people only stay long enough for the doctors and nurses to test out which drug works (or semi-works), and then they kick the patients out within a week so they can give up their beds to other "crazy people."

When I was in the residential clinic, I had strict rules and consequences whenever I engaged in an eating behavior or habit that I wasn't supposed to, such as purge in the bathroom, refuse to follow strict meal plans, or skip group therapies. I was closely monitored at every step, making it difficult to rebel.

In the inpatient hospital, however, I had complete freedom…surprisingly. Other than having a nurse come in every morning to draw my blood, measure my heart-rate, and make sure I wasn't going to kill myself that day, I was able to do whatever I wanted. I was able to choose my breakfasts, lunches, and dinners from a list of options (I was even given the option of not eating at all), and no one stopped me when my food choices were clearly disordered.

I ate plain Cheerios for breakfast and plain lettuce for lunch and dinner. No one stopped me when I immediately went into the bathroom afterward to purge. No one came into my room and forced me to attend group therapy even when I skipped every single one.

Shamefully Vanished
A Memoir of a Girl Out of Control

My eating disorder became even more out of control, as I felt that it was okay to binge and purge in a fucking hospital. Messed up, right!? However, even though I was able to get away with it during that time, the doctors and nurses knew what I was up to, as they refused to let me check out until I was immediately able to check back into the residential clinic I had JUST been discharged from.

One night, while I was preoccupied with my nightly purge of half-digested lettuce while pretending to take a shower, I heard a loud scream followed by at least twenty people mumbling simultaneously. I stepped out of the bathroom and saw a crowd of nurses and patients lingering in front of my room.

The schizophrenic and suicidal girl, whose room was across from mine, had stabbed herself with a filed-down pencil until she bled to death. She could not have been more than 19-years old, and if she had been discovered sooner rather than only when they came around for nightly checks, she could have still been alive.

I watched medics come in, put her on a gurney, and wheeled her out. She had spent the last eight years of her life in and out of psychiatric hospitals, barely having a chance to live her life. That incident should have changed my way of thinking.

That traumatic moment should have steered me away from my depressed thoughts forever, motivating me to want to recover and live life before it's too late. However, despite the situation, I felt emotionless from it. Watching someone die didn't seem to affect me at all, as I went back into my own room, closed the door, and continued purging.

Shamefully Vanished
A Memoir of a Girl Out of Control

Chapter Fourteen
Second Residential Experience

My second time at the residential clinic went much smoother than my first. Since I had already been there less than two months ago, I felt like a senior member. I knew the rules. I knew the ropes. I knew the tips and tricks to get them to discharge me and provide full consent to my school before I was actually ready to be discharged.

I knew how to bullshit through meal levels and get to the point where I can choose my own food, and I knew how to secretly exercise and purge (food included, not

Shamefully Vanished
A Memoir of a Girl Out of Control

just supplements) in my room without getting caught. I had manipulated the counselors into trusting me by pretending to follow the rules and pretending to do everything right.

Little did they know, I had purged and stuffed coins in my underwear for "weight gain" for the entire five weeks I was there. I snuck in Splenda during my trips out and gave them to other residents. (To those with eating disorders, Splenda is heaven. It's the delicious sugary taste, the feeling of actually eating something, without all the added calories. It's so good that we like to pretend that it doesn't cause cancer).

I made it seem like I was getting better by the day when really, I was only getting better at pretending and hiding. I threw up every day during my second time around, losing weight and hiding food in between my clothes and inside my socks without anyone suspecting a thing.

I also did sit ups in my room as I didn't have a roommate to catch me in the act. Even if I did, the residents covered for each other all the time regardless, aiding one another in their own personal sickness.

I didn't know at the time that I was only wasting my parents' money and hurting myself by faking my recovery. To me, it was only another thing that I was able to control in my life when it seemed out of control otherwise.

Not only did I fake my way through weight checks and meals, I also knew that the quickest way to get back into school and into classes was to convince my therapist that my dysfunctional living situation at home was the main reason I felt depressed and needed to turn to my eating disorder.

My therapist scheduled a family therapy session, but beforehand, I convinced my therapist that my mother was the main reason I felt dysfunctional, fully knowing that my therapist would question my mother, and fully knowing that my mother would be resistant and start verbally attacking my therapist, convincing my therapist that I truly needed to get out of the house.

I was so determined to keep my disorder and still get back into school that I became an expert at turning everyone against each other, just so I wouldn't have to actually recover. I had turned my parents' lives upside down, but at that time, I didn't care. All I cared about was myself.

Shamefully Vanished
A Memoir of a Girl Out of Control

Chapter Fifteen
Chugging and Change

It's done. My plan worked as I had expected. Upon discharge from residential, my therapist and psychiatrist sent a note to my dean that I was ready to go back to school. I had to pass one last check, a final weigh-in from my school nurse to double check the clinic's numbers.

I was prepared. I knew exactly what I had to do. I was so close to getting back onto campus that I refused to let anything stand in the way.

Shamefully Vanished
A Memoir of a Girl Out of Control

My mother and I drove over two hours to get to campus for my weight check. I was still severely underweight, and my mother knew that I was not physically ready to return.

To cover up my boney ribs and chest, I layered up in clothing where I could, such as my underwear, socks, and I added extra-weighted padding in my bra, as I knew I would have to strip down to my undergarments and get into a hospital gown.

I also shoved a bag of quarters in my underwear, securing it tight with rubber bands so the quarters didn't jingle or fall loose when I moved. To top it off, I chugged an entire gallon of water before walking onto the scale, adding fifteen pounds when I stepped on.

My mother knew all my tricks, and she knew that I was trying to cover up my true weight, but she was also desperate to get me back into school that she actually encouraged my actions. The nurses were fooled. The dean was fooled, and three weeks later, I moved my belongings back onto campus.

Despite being back on campus, I was still put on probation. I had two conditions to abide by if I wanted to stay in school. One, I had to attend weight checks every week to ensure that I was maintaining my "healthy weight." And two, I had to attend group therapy once a week to "talk about my feelings" and "gain support from my peers."

I continued to fake my weight during weight checks by shoving coins in my underwear and chugging water.

Shamefully Vanished
A Memoir of a Girl Out of Control

During group therapies, I either stayed silent or gave bullshit answers that were always lies when I was forced to speak.

***

Group therapy was pointless and always a waste of the hour I could have been using for more important things like binging and purging. Group therapy consisted of a bunch of people with problems sitting around, either whining endlessly about nothing or refusing to say how they really felt.

We were all afraid to speak up on what was really going on with us, for the fear that one wrong word would create a forced medical leave. We also had to pretend like we cared about the sessions by participating, aka, giving cliché advices to others that we don't believe in ourselves.

I had a single dorm room when I went back to campus, with one communal bathroom that was shared among the entire hall of twenty different residents rather than a private bathroom. I knew I wouldn't be able to purge in a bathroom with that many people around, people who would eventually suspect something and rat me out. Plus, I could no longer purge in the bath tub as I had done before I left campus because well…there were no bath tubs.

So, I resorted to binging AND purging in my dorm room. Rather than purging in toilets and bath tubs like "normal bulimics," I stole garbage bags and rolls of paper towels from maintenance, used the bags to cover my laundry hamper, lined the bags with paper towels to provide absorption and to prevent splash back, and then vomited inside the bags.

I don't know why I was so motivated to get back into school. During my absence, I became anxious about wasting my tuition and ruining my life if I didn't get back into classes. Now that I was back in, it didn't seem like any of that anxiety had an effect.

Similar to the last time I was on campus, I continued to skip classes, and I spent all my time either binging in the cafeteria or ordering delivery and binging on those, purging them all out into garbage bags. I then tied the bags up and threw them out in the communal trash cans in the hallway. I continued this for two months, thinking I was brilliant with my improvisations, until my dean caught on.

She brought me into her office one day to "check in with me," while casually mentioning that "bags of vomit" were found in the communal hall of my building, and she asked if I knew anything about it or about who was doing it since it "wasn't my style" to vomit into bags. Fuck the truth. I was done telling the truth in attempts to "save myself from myself."

So, I lied my ass off. I pretended like I had no idea what she was talking about while my heart began to sink as I wasn't sure whether she was able to read through my words of lies. However, she didn't question me further about the issue, but I knew I had to be sneakier.

I continued to binge in my room and purge inside garbage bags, but I could no longer throw them out in the hallway trash cans. Instead, I tied up the bags of vomit, shoved them into the biggest backpack I could find, and walked off campus to throw them out in community trash cans and dumpsters in the middle of the night, where no one would suspect a thing.

I never got caught. It was a genius plan despite the breach in safety during the night times in that area, especially as a single female. Regrettably, I was forced to leave school again after that one semester back because I had failed to chug enough water during that last weight check, and I was two pounds under my goal weight. TWO. FUCKING. POUNDS. Two damn pounds for another indefinite nightmare of hell.

Shamefully Vanished
A Memoir of a Girl Out of Control

Chapter Sixteen
My Living Hell

During my second forced medical leave, I felt as if my school had given up on me. They no longer tried to get me into a clinic. They no longer tried to get me help. I was left alone. I was abandoned.

I was only told to stay at home and send weekly updates on my weight to the school nurse. If I was able to maintain my weight on my own, then, and only then, would I be allowed back on campus.

Shamefully Vanished
A Memoir of a Girl Out of Control

By that point, everyone around me had grown tired of my "antics." They were expensing so much time and energy on me and viewed me as not even trying in my recovery. My dean no longer cared whether I could get back onto campus, and I was beginning to feel like I had flunk out of school.

People get held back in kindergarten for not being emotionally ready to begin first grade. I got held back for not being emotionally ready for college. I felt like a failure. I was a failure. I wanted to look like nothingness, and instead, I became nothingness.

I became more depressed than ever. The first three months moving back in with my parents', again, I continued to binge and purge. I had accepted that this was now my life, and I would never be able to go back to school.

Even if I miraculously overcame this disease, with my track record, I wouldn't end up graduating until I was 30. I had given up. I spent all my days eating, throwing up, and pretending to go on walks so I could throw up the dinners that my parents forced me to eat into my neighbors' shrubs.

One dark afternoon, after an endless three weeks of self-loathing, while my parents were at work, I took a sharp razor blade and carved the words "HELP ME" onto my abdomen. I had just finished my 32nd purge of the day and wanted the nightmare that was my life to be over.

Shamefully Vanished
A Memoir of a Girl Out of Control

I tried brushing it off like I had done nothing wrong when my parents came home, pretending that I had just spent the day job-hunting. Binging and purging made me feel almost bipolar. One minute, I was at a high, hoarding food and hiding my secret, and the next, I was at a low, hating my body and wanting to die.

Later that night, I began having spontaneous heart palpitations. I tried to sleep them off like I had done when my diet pills almost gave me a heart attack. However, I couldn't, and the events that followed that moment led to one of the worst experiences in my life.

After lying in bed for 45-minutes, unable to breathe or speak, I painfully crawled out into the living room, where my parents were watching TV, and I signaled to them that I needed help as I couldn't speak. They freaked out and bellowed to my brother to get dressed so they could all take me to the nearest emergency room.

After three hours of waiting and comprehensive tests, the doctor's consensus (after $800 of unnecessary work) was that I was just dehydrated. However, they did find the "HELP ME" carved onto my abdomen and refused to let me go home, insisting that I signed a voluntary consent to check into a psychiatric facility for adults instead.

Another psychiatric facility, I thought, all because I released more water from my body than I had put in. Still hooked onto an IV, I resentfully signed my freedom away. Two hours later, an ambulance pulled up and took me to the closest psychiatric hospital. They didn't trust my parents to drive me straight there, so instead, my family had to shell out $4,000 just for a stupid 20-minute car ride.

I was taken to the closest psychiatric facility in the area, the one located in the dark part of the city, the one known for its brutal employee handling, forced lockdowns, and cramped living spaces. This hospital had been rumored to torture their patients for not abiding by the protocols and for keeping them locked up for much longer than expected.

Foolishly, I assumed that I would be able to sign a 72-hour notice after checking in, only having to stay in the hell-hole for three days, and satisfying those around me in that I would be "better" upon discharge. That was the only reason I signed myself in voluntarily. So, I could sign myself out voluntarily. Little did I know, those three days quickly turned into six weeks.

***

Life inside that psychiatric hospital was my worst experience to date. Upon arrival, I walked through three guarded gates with heavy security just to enter the building. I then walked through a metal detector and signed myself in, getting assigned a number like a prisoner so the hospital could keep track of its patients. There were so many patients there that it made it difficult for nurses to become personable to the sick and diseased, and instead, treated them like scumbags and experimented on them like lab rats.

After nearly six hours of waiting, a nurse, who barely looked like he graduated from college, came down to prepare me for my new life inside "the box." He had a male security guard pat me down and dress me in a hospital gown (which probably was against hospital policy), and I had to put all my belongings, phone and wallet included, inside a plastic bag for them to keep hold of so I wouldn't be able to hurt myself with anything. Sure, let me just cut myself with a dollar bill. Serial killers do that all the time. Super effective!

I then had less than five minutes to say my parting words to my parents before I was escorted through four more high-security metal doors and into a run-down unit with two nurses wheeling out a screaming and cursing man in his 40s, strapped down to a gurney. I was in prison. I was inmate 236.

Everyone in there was old. They also all looked like they haven't showered in months. At least when I was in residential and the other inpatient hospital, there were people my age, or at least, people who were clean, even if only a couple. All the patients in this hospital were at least twenty years older than me, and I felt like I didn't belong. I felt scared. Alone, once again.

I was escorted to my room, a dark and windowless space with nothing but a small metal table and a small creaky bed. My bathroom was connected to the room next to mine, with only a thin curtain to separate the toilets and a shared shower. My bathroom neighbor was an old and obese man with chronic health conditions and schizophrenia, who constantly tried to peek at me whenever I used the toilet. After a few times, I settled for pissing in a bucket next to my bed.

Shamefully Vanished
A Memoir of a Girl Out of Control

I walked out to the main lobby, sat down on the worn-out couch, picked up the romance novel sitting beside me, and looked around. Everyone was half-dressed and slept on the dirty floor, wrapped in blankets while shivering and mumbling to themselves or carving into the wooden tables with their fingernails.

What the hell was this place? I did not want to be there. For the first time since I developed my eating disorder, I actually felt fear. I kept telling myself that I would be out in three days. Three days. That's it. That did not quell my fear.

The next morning, I sprung out of bed and ran to the nurse's station to sign my 72-hour notice. I wanted to sign it the night I arrived, but they refused to let me as the front desk closed at 5pm, and I had to wait until the next morning.

To my surprise, they STILL refused to let me sign it. They insisted that I would have to wait another two days before I could sign anything because the doctors wanted to put me on an anti-depressive medication. Because the medication was new to me, the nurses would need to monitor my blood pressure and look out for any side effects before I could be released from their care.

Reluctantly, I agreed, signing my life away for another 48-hours. I continued with my daily routine. For someone who hated losing control of her life, I found myself in a lot of situations where that became the case, first in residential, and now here.

Shamefully Vanished
A Memoir of a Girl Out of Control

Every day, I woke up at the crack of dawn to an obese nurse, who noisily wheeled in a machine to check my vitals. I then walked down the hall to stand in a long line with sick patients who waited to receive their medications from a window slit.

I ate a shitty breakfast of toast with butter, sat around while hearing old people cough and complain about their lives, ate a shitty lunch of bread and deli meat, took a nap until dinnertime, ate a shitty dinner of bland and disgusting chicken, and sat around watching people go insane as I got in trouble for dressing provocatively and distracting the other patients from their recovery.

I wore a t-shirt and shorts that reached down to my knees. How was that provocative? Besides, was it really my fault that people had so little self-control that they couldn't stop leering at other patients?

Despite sharing a bathroom with an obese and sexually-charged man, I continued to binge and purge all my meals. I became so depressed in that hospital that even the thought of binging and purging no longer excited me. However, I continued to do so as I needed to gain control back of my own life somehow.

***

Two days later, I attempted to sign the 72-hour notice again, only to be met with another rebuttal. This time, I was told that the medication they had put me on was not showing any signs of improvement, and that I would be put on a new medication, a medication that would take another week to monitor its progress.

Shamefully Vanished
A Memoir of a Girl Out of Control

Another. Fucking. Week. I was beginning to get frustrated. The three days I had originally agreed to quickly turned into two weeks, with nothing but false hope in sight remaining.

A week after being tested again like a lab rat, I attempted to sign yet another notice. To no one's surprise, I was still refused. Instead, I was told that the medication needed yet ANOTHER TWO WEEKS in order to stabilize, and that they could not, in good conscience, allow me to leave without constant monitoring by a professional.

I even suggested continuing my vital checks at my family doctor and sending them the reports, which they responded with distaste.

Despite what I did or said, they fought with me every step of the way. It no longer mattered if I was an adult. I had the rights to sign myself in because I was an adult, but once they got me to put my name onto the paper, I was stuck. I lost my right to sign myself out. They refused to acknowledge my voluntary notice to leave because they deemed that I was mentally unfit to make safe and conscious decisions for myself.

They even refused to allow my parents to sign me out because I was legally an adult, and my parents no longer had a say in my medical decisions. I was also told that if I continued to insist on leaving, the hospital would be forced to take me to court on the count of "mental psychosis," causing me to lose thousands of dollars and allowing the hospital to gain full control of me.

Shamefully Vanished
A Memoir of a Girl Out of Control

Really? Mental psychosis? If I wasn't "crazy" enough before I went into the hospital, hearing the term "mental psychosis" really made me lose my nerves. I flipped out. I became psychotic and insane.

I grabbed my nurse's clipboard and threw it against the barricaded metal doors, attempting to kick and scream my way out. I went over to the tables in the lobby and erratically kicked off all the board games and books as I started knocking chairs over two by two. I was a mess. I became what the hospital saw me as. A mental patient.

I became erratic and unstable. It wasn't until I almost harmed another patient with my chaotic behaviors that I was restrained by two nurses, who tied me up in a straightjacket and bolted me inside my room for five days, no freedom, no visitors, no contact with anyone or anything, with a feeding tube stuck inside of me as I had lost the ability to use my hands.

My six weeks of hell in that facility could have only been four if I didn't freak out like I had. However, being locked in closed quarters with no hope or end in sight is enough to make any sane person become psychotic. It was not a safe and attentive place like the other hospitals I had been in. It was cold, and the employees did not care about anyone except for their paychecks.

Patients were ripping their hairs out in public and no one cared to stop them. Hour after hour, I saw people breaking down and talking about how depressed they were, only to be met with a lockdown inside their rooms and no mental support. I met people who had been

Shamefully Vanished
A Memoir of a Girl Out of Control

trapped in there for decades because the doctors there associated any kind of "negative" emotions with "insanity."

Because of my brutal experience, being locked inside that hospital made me swore to myself that I would never put myself in the position of having to stay in a psychiatric hospital ever again.

Shamefully Vanished
A Memoir of a Girl Out of Control

Shamefully Vanished
A Memoir of a Girl Out of Control

Chapter Seventeen
The Phase Never Ended

After a year of bouncing back and forth between hospitals and home, I faked my way back onto campus once again by stuffing my pants, chugging gallons, and lying my ass off.

All the issues that I had before I left campus for the first time were all still there when I came back. I made friends, found love, and even aced my way to graduation during my last two years, but the binging and purging never stopped.

Shamefully Vanished
A Memoir of a Girl Out of Control

I was happy on the outside but still living in misery and despair on the inside, continuing to hold my secrets and refusing to let any part of the past three years of my life out into the public...until now.

My eating disorder lasted for over five years during college and continued for another five years after. I can't even honestly say that I'm not still struggling to this day. After graduation, I moved into my own apartment, spending over $1,500 a month JUST so I could have the privacy of binging and purging without the need to hide.

I had deceived enough people into thinking that I was better, and that I no longer needed to be locked under someone else's key. I had learned the hard way that the truth only served to bite me in the ass, and that it was better to lie in my shame alone.

Whenever I felt slightly stressed, sad, or bored, I found myself locked inside my apartment for days at a time, binging and purging on the many bags of junk food I bought from the closest grocery store, hoarding chips, cookies, and tasty cakes as they were the easiest food to expel from my body.

I ordered delivery over six times a week, each time with enough food to feed a party of twelve, blasted my music to pretend that I was having a party, and binged on everything I ordered in one sitting, from Chinese food to pizza to hoagies to fast food, within the time span of eight hours, only taking a break to purge.

Because I no longer needed to hide my bulimic habits, I became a non-stop binging machine, purging so much

Shamefully Vanished
A Memoir of a Girl Out of Control

and so often that my enamel began to wear out and my gums began to recede.

I had learned a trick during residential to swig my mouth with mouth wash after every purge, rather than brush my teeth, to protect my teeth from rapid enamel erosion. However, this trick only works if you're not actively throwing up over thirty times a day like I had been.

I moved in with my then-partner a year after graduation, hoping that it would be the kick I needed to finally stop my habits. However, rather than stopping, I continued to binge and purge, binging out in the open while locking myself in the bathroom and blasting music to cover up the gagging and multiple toilet flushes from my purges.

To this day, I am still not sure if my partner ever suspected anything, but regardless, he never mentioned a word, and that feeling of power made me continue. For bulimics, shame is a powerful motivator to stop. The four dreaded words of "Did you throw up?" is enough to make any bulimic either want to stop for good or cover their tracks more.

My biggest downfall, the moment that made me question what I was doing and increased my motivation to stop, was the night I binged and purged on molding burgers, questionable shakes that smelled like baby barf, and my own vomit behind a shady fast-food restaurant.

I had just engaged in a brutal and epic fight with my partner, and I stormed out of the apartment as a result.

Shamefully Vanished
A Memoir of a Girl Out of Control

The intense stress and anger that I felt from the argument made me crave a binge and purge session. Binging and purging was difficult to do in public to begin with, and especially harder without a wallet.

It was a dark night, with rain pouring from the cloudy sky. I trudged through the night, walking three miles to the only fast-food burger chain restaurant that was semi-isolated in my part of town. I went behind the building and found their dumpster.

By this point, I had become an expert at pigging out behind dumpsters, eating more of my meals there than I had anywhere else over the past eight years.

These dumpsters were usually gold mines, as fast-food restaurants tend to overestimate how much food they actually need per day so they "cook" more than they sell, throwing out the leftovers at the end of the day when they realized that they had overcooked.

I had been to this spot before. I had scoped it out days earlier and made sure that it had low traffic and was police-free. I was excited. I could smell the stench from fifty feet away, and despite the liquefying odor, my salivary glands began to activate. The thrill of knowing that I would soon be able to dive into that dumpster and pull out bags and bags of burgers and fries sent shivers down my spine.

When I was in the midst of my bulimia, my logic and common sense didn't exist when it came to what I liked to call my "sessions." My sole focus on stuffing and vomiting clouded my ability to see exactly what I was eating and where I was eating it.

During those moments, I would eat anything, anything that I was able to chew or swallow (those were often mutually exclusive), whether or not they resembled food, and I couldn't care less where I was while doing it.

I reached my arm inside the dumpster, bypassing the stench and flies, grabbed two large garbage bags, and pulled them out, heaving and almost falling over in the process. I sneakily ran into the bushes behind the dumpster with my bags, behaving as if I had just robbed a bank. I checked my surroundings to ensure that no one could see me before diving into my bags of "goodies."

I enthusiastically tore open one of the bags and was immediately smacked in the face by a huge wave of odor. Unlike some of my other dumpster-diving nights, I was not adorned with half-fresh, half-stale burgers.

Instead, I came face-to-face with moldy burgers and liquefying fries as I unveiled the contents of the bag, not realizing that this restaurant had to close early due to lack of power, causing everything to turn rotten. I tried the other bag, only to become overpowered by the same stench and odor. There were over a hundred burgers in those bags; not a single one was semi-fresh.

Part of me was disgusted with what I saw, and I wanted to throw the bags back into the dumpster and call it quits. However, the stronger part of me felt my stomach growl as I hadn't eaten all day. My strong desire for binging and purging overpowered my distaste for possible diseases and illnesses.

Covering my nostrils, I reached in and grabbed a handful of fries, shoving them into my mouth as my taste buds became overwhelmed with salt and other questionable flavors.

The taste of food, regardless of how nauseating it was, made me crave for more. I started eating the burgers, picking the mold off them and shoving the rest down my throat. I didn't stop to breathe. I ate and ate until I began to feel sick.

More than fifty burgers later, I stood up, walked behind a nearby tree, and threw the burgers and fries up, returning to the bags to polish off the rest before returning home.

* * *

To this day, I am still not "recovered" from my eating disorder. Although I am no longer actively binging and purging nonstop, I still have moments where I feel like I have eaten too much, and I force myself to throw up. I have identified that the more stressed out I feel, the more I resort to binging and purging as my source of comfort. All the dysfunctional thoughts that I had during my worst moments are all still there; I have just managed to silence them in a more controllable manner.

I continue to binge and purge whenever I feel alone and sad, or whenever I feel heavier and thicker than I would like. Rather than resorting to diet and exercise like

Shamefully Vanished
A Memoir of a Girl Out of Control

most people, I resort to binging and purging because, from experience, I know that binging and purging allows me to eat what I want and not gain weight. It has been over 10 years since my eating disorder began, and I do not foresee it coming to an end any time soon.

I wish I could say I recovered from my eating disorder, but like most people who struggled or still struggle, does it really ever end?

Shamefully Vanished
A Memoir of a Girl Out of Control

Chapter Eighteen
Shame

When it comes to eating disorders, for me at least, there is a lot of effort that gets put into concealing the secret and doing everything possible to avoid getting caught and exposed.

Having this "secret" is the only thing we feel we have left, and even though the actions we engage in while in the midst of it are debilitating and embarrassing, we still see them as "better" than having our secrets discovered and taken away from us. We are terrified of being forced to relinquish control of the one "accomplishment" we are proud of.

However, that sense of power and accomplishment in keeping the secret is also what makes the sick remain sick. We become so ashamed of telling the truth because, all our lives, we have had to be "perfect" and always had to do the right thing.

We cannot handle the embarrassment that comes with having people find out that we are not as put together as we pretend we are. Even if we strive to be honest, we cannot deal with the disgrace that comes with telling people that we purposefully starve ourselves or that we deliberately throw up after every meal because we don't want to get "fat." We can't. No one will take us seriously, and no one will believe that we do not have control over these actions.

To this day, the term "fat" is still associated with shallow and external appearances, body physique, and a lack of control when it comes to eating and hunger. We use the term loosely, calling those who are larger than others "fat," and we are afraid of getting "fat" so we over-exercise and under-eat.

However, for those with eating disorders, the term "fat" becomes more about failure and a loss of control, something more internal rather than external.

Those immersed in the diseases we call "eating disorders" know that the term "fat" means something completely different than the popular concept. Getting "fat," to us, no longer means becoming wider in size and heavier in weight. Getting "fat" means relinquishing control over the one part of life we thought we could finally call "ours."

Gaining 5lbs means that we have allowed ourselves to slip and fail in our goals. We become heavier in our self-hatred and self-disappointment, seeing even a miniscule weight gain as a call for self-destruction and the end of the world.

People with eating disorders already experience self-loathing and self-regret. We know our behaviors are destructive and that we should stop, but we don't. We can't. We develop this dichotomous thinking, a black and white mindset, where we experience ultimate failure if circumstances do not go our way.

We cannot simply eat without eating everything. We cannot simply diet without resorting to extreme diets of under 500 calories a day. We cannot simply purge once without experiencing the guilt that we must continue purging or else we will gain 10lbs overnight.

We engage in eating disorder symptoms and immediately regret our actions, but we continue anyway, because the actions we regret are the same actions that keep us strong and distracted.

Unlike the stigma that comes with drug addictions, eating addictions are seen as repugnant, disgusting, and only associated with overweight people. We still do not accept that eating disorders are diseases because, unlike drug or alcohol addictions where chemicals physically interfere with our brains, eating disorders are "just about wanting to lose weight" or "just a way for shallow people to gain attention."

Eating disorders are also one of the most difficult mental disorders to overcome. Those addicted to drugs and alcohol can just cut their usage out completely, which creates a whole myriad of withdrawal symptoms, but at least they'll still survive.

Those who suffer from eating disorders cannot completely cut out their drug of choice because they physically need it to survive. How do we recover from a drug when that same drug is needed to live?

How can we come clean about a disease when one, it's not socially acceptable and still has misconceptions around it, and two, being honest makes it even worse than staying silent? How do we stop something when stopping also means potentially dying?

Bulimia Nervosa and shame often go hand in hand, where those affected often feel like they are less worthy of life than others around them. They tend to see themselves as "worthless," with a perceived lower status compared to others, and therefore, lack the motivation to recover.

They also lack the motivation to recover in that, although binging and purging is viewed as a sense of gaining control, it is also viewed as a sense of losing self-control, where bulimics become envious of how those around them can suppress their urges to not binge while they cannot, how those around them can just eat a simple

Shamefully Vanished
A Memoir of a Girl Out of Control

meal and stop while they have to go on a rampage and eat everything in sight.

This external and internal shame force them to hold onto their secret because they cannot allow others to see them as "not good enough" or having a "lack of self-control." Essentially, bulimics believe they are not worthy of recovery.

Intense feelings of shame create further isolation and a self-perception of failure. These feelings force those with any types of eating disorder, not just bulimia, to become warped in a constant cycle of destructive (and sometimes illegal) behavior and self-regret.

They engage in their eating behaviors to relieve the shame they feel internally, and they experience intense feelings of shame when they engage in their eating behaviors, creating a mental paradox.

What tends to begin as a way to gain back control of life can quickly turn into spiraling out of control. When tends to begin as an innocent plan to feel powerful can quickly spiral into a psychological battle within the mind.

People who struggle with eating disorders are predominantly controlled by the power of the superego, the tyrannical voice that seeks to prevent the natural instincts and behaviors of the id.

For example, when the id cries out, "I'm hungry," the superego takes over and forces the affected person to experience the message of, "You will never be loved or worthy if you don't lose any weight! You're not allowed to take another bite until you lose 50lbs!"

Because the id plays a crucial role in human survival, the perfectionism that comes with eating disorders takes away that role in order to satisfy the unrealistic expectations of the superego, resulting in "tolerable" and continual self-starvation.

We can see the constant battle between the id and the superego in bulimic behaviors. The id causes bulimics to feel hungry and want to eat, leading to a full-blown binge because the hunger instinct has been repressed for too long.

However, the superego tries to combat this by preventing the id from allowing us to keep the food in, creating this mindset of "if we want to eat, we must get rid of it," so we purge, allowing us to satisfy the needs of both the id and the superego.

Shamefully Vanished
A Memoir of a Girl Out of Control

Chapter Nineteen
Mind-Body Disconnection

Eating disorders create a psychological mind-body disconnection, where the body reacts in ways that are out of the mind's conscious awareness, for example, how logic and common sense are lost during periods of self-starvation.

On the external level, we want to stop. We want nothing more than to stop engaging in these physically painful behaviors that put us at risk of death. We tell ourselves that we will stop purging. We tell ourselves that we will eat "normally." We tell ourselves that we will finally be disorder-free for a change…starting tomorrow. Always starting tomorrow.

This is because our bodies reject our mindsets and create an out-of-mind experience where we continue to purge and starve regardless of what we tell ourselves, so we give into our cravings, unaware that we are engaging in these actions until we are already too deep in them.

Body dysmorphia is a prime example of mind-body disconnection, where we perceive ourselves as having one appearance while actually having another appearance. We perceive our bodies in dimensions that we fear becoming, such as perceiving ourselves as overweight and obese even as we are whittling away into nothingness.

Our self-neglect and self-hatred have created intense and irrational fears where we cannot physically see the dimensions that we truly are, only the dimensions we perceive in our minds.

There is a common misbelief that people with eating disorders are shallow, and that they purposefully starve themselves just to lose weight. However, eating disorders are more about self-loathing than about vanity. Eating disorders become an out-of-body experience when victims are immersed in it.

When I was in the midst of my eating disorder, I completely lost control of my thoughts and actions. It felt like there was a drive pushing me to behave in ways I didn't want to, and I believed that there would be consequences if I didn't abide.

Shamefully Vanished
A Memoir of a Girl Out of Control

Like many sufferers, my eating disorder started off as a means to take back control of my own life. After my fallout in a situation I could not control, I saw an opportunity to control my body and the food I put into it, so I did.

The satisfaction of writing down every ounce and every nutritional chemical I was putting inside of me made me feel like I had a purpose, so when I lost it and began binging, I became depressed, while continuing to hold my emotions inside my exploding brain.

That's why purging was so satisfying for me. When I purged, it felt like all my problems, all the emotions that had been trapped inside my mind, were all coming out at once. It was a sense of relief that I felt I couldn't achieve through any other means.

For me, binging and purging became my coping mechanism for the emotions that I wasn't allowed to feel. It was a way of shoving down all my problems just to let them all out at once and watch them wash away. I did not purge because I wanted to binge more. I binged because there were moments where I felt like I needed to purge, and therefore, I binged.

My eating disorder shifted me from someone with goals and ambition to someone with constant urges and thoughts revolving food. I went through years where the only thing I could focus on was food. I developed more relationships with food than I did with people.

I became angry when food was taken away from me as it became my source of security. Over a decade of my

Shamefully Vanished
A Memoir of a Girl Out of Control

life revolved around eating, not eating, purging, not purging, and there were days where I wished it all went away.

Don't get me wrong; it's not like I haven't tried to stop. I have. Many times. I have thought about how maybe I really had control over my eating disorder but every time I tried to control it, I failed epically.

I have tried throwing away all my food to avoid binging, just to end up picking them out of the trash and eating them. I have tried leaving my apartment to avoid the craving of wanting to binge and purge, only to find myself binging and purging in public.

I have tried spending money on other things so I could leave myself with nothing left to spend on food, only to find myself going into debt by also continuing to order delivery.

I have tried so many times to overcome this disease, including going to therapy and overdosing on Seroquel, as Seroquel is supposed to suppress your appetite. I have tried eating normal meals and distracting myself from the mind that causes me to engage in my episodes, but I end up failing every single time.

Bulimia kept me from feeling alone and isolated in a world where I felt like no one cared. Bulimia kept me safe and gave me something to rely on. It is actually a lot harder and more dangerous to be bulimic than to be anorexic because no one ever notices that you're sick if you don't look sickly underweight, and the constant pressure of your stomach acid pushing up against your esophagus creates deadly risks for intestinal ruptures.

There is no quick fix for Bulimia Nervosa. I have tried every trick in the book, and I have spent thousands of dollars on therapies and self-help books. The only tried and true method that ever worked for me, even if only temporarily, was being around people 24/7, people who knew my habits and kept me grounded whenever I felt an episode coming. It just required the extra push from myself to step out of my dungeon of isolation and anti-socialism.

The fear of being caught is a bulimic's worst nightmare, and if there is a constant fear that someone is always coming, the habit begins to eventually subside. To this day, I still binge and purge. I am not recovered. Far from it. As long as I continue to suffer internally, my actions will reveal it.

Shamefully Vanished
A Memoir of a Girl Out of Control

Chapter Twenty
Keeping Secrets

"You are only as sick as your secrets."

Our secrets drain us of our souls and psychological energies, which can result in a variety of mental disorders such as anxiety and depression as we try, but fail, to compensate. This is especially the case when it comes to holding onto secrets related to the self as opposed to holding onto secrets related to external situations or others.

Shamefully Vanished
A Memoir of a Girl Out of Control

Holding onto a secret is not as simple as not speaking or not being honest. Those who suffer from eating disorders hold onto secrets that they wish others would discover. It becomes physically and mentally draining when we want to share a secret about ourselves but feel we are unable to. This leads us to fight a constant battle with ourselves on a whole myriad of questions on why we continue to hold onto these secrets even as they are killing us, why we are so concerned with being exposed when millions of others deal with the same struggles, and why we become so fearful of others when we are our biggest critics.

This back-and-forth battle with ourselves is what keeps us socially isolated from others, cautious of any sort of interaction for the fear of being exposed or accidentally revealing a secret. We start to become antisocial and alone because we believe intimacy creates an opportunity for exposure.

Slowly, we begin to give up aspects of our lives that risk our secrets from being publicized, eventually becoming paranoid and associating any sort of laughter or conversation between strangers with them knowing about our secrets.

However, secrets are only psychologically tormenting when they are about the self, when they are tied to our feelings and our emotions. This is because people often view their secrets as being unique to them, and if these "unique secrets" were to become unveiled, they would be seen as social outcasts and "different."

Shamefully Vanished
A Memoir of a Girl Out of Control

No one wants to be different, unoriginal. We filter what we share with others and only allow them to know the secrets that we want them to know rather than the secrets that we need them to know.

Because of this, the more we hold onto our secrets, the lower our self-esteems become as we feel less content with ourselves and with our social connections, always feeling like we are left out of the circle because we can never expose our true selves, always wearing a mask to conceal the persona we hide beneath.

Shamefully Vanished
A Memoir of a Girl Out of Control

Shamefully Vanished
A Memoir of a Girl Out of Control

A true story of a girl who became trapped inside her own body.

Shamefully Vanished
A Memoir of a Girl Out of Control

Shamefully Vanished
A Memoir of a Girl Out of Control

Shamefully Vanished
A Memoir of a Girl Out of Control

www.ingramcontent.com/pod-product-compliance
Lightning Source LLC
Chambersburg PA
CBHW021152080526
44588CB00008B/303